The Lazy Man's Guide to Death & Dying

by

E. J. Gold

The Lazy Man's Guide to Death & Dying

by

E. J. Gold

IDHHB, Inc.
Publishers
1983

First Printing: March, 1984
Second Printing: August, 1984

Published by:
IDHHB, INC.
PO BOX 370
Nevada City, CA 95959

Some material in this book has appeared previously under the
title: *New American Book of the Dead,* © 1981.

Cover Painting & Original Drawings: Thomas Johnson
Cover Design: Nancy Christie
Typesetting & Paste-up: Wayne Hoyle

ISBN: 0-89556-042-9

INTRODUCTION

The Lazy Man's Guide to Death and Dying is a very interesting series of programs to facilitate the process of dying and to insure that one can reincarnate or not reincarnate as one chooses.

This is a very difficult discipline and the book is very specific on the various steps and stages towards achieving this goal.

Those of us who are older, I am 69, are very interested in these processes, the imminence of death brings one up short, one realizes the inevitability and the necessity of doing something about it.

I highly recommend this book to those who can find an interest in the subject and recommend to those who are not interested to become interested. Best of luck with your own explorations.

John C. Lilly, M.D.,
author of *Center of the Cyclone*

PREFACE

A spiritual classic that will rank even higher than the **Upanishads,** *the* **Koran,** *the* **Odyssey, Crime and Punishment,** *or* **Elephant Doody Comix.**

With this book E.J. Gold joins the company of cosmic liberators along with Buddha, Lao-Tse, Nasrudin, Christian Rosycross and W.C. Fields.

Absolutely indispensible for anyone planning to die in the next five hundred years. Those not planning to die should also read it, since one is likely to encounter these experiences anyway if one experiments with yoga, Encounter Groups, sneaky Sufis or certain Controlled Substances.

This book confirms my suspicion that E.J. Gold is a genius.

The passages about the central source of all phenomena and the young lady from Wooster are alone worth the price of the book.

Robert Anton Wilson,
author of *Cosmic Trigger* and *Schrödinger's Cat*

TABLE OF CONTENTS

PROLOGUE

The King's New Klothes: An Ancient Myth

Once — and only once — many years ago, so long ago even the passage of time had not yet begun, there was a King who was so fond of new clothes that He spent everything He had on them.

He had a different costume for every hour in the day, every day in the week, and every week in the year...

Nothing mattered to Him except His clothes; yet He was not satisfied with all the splendor of His wardrobe. Whenever His tailor came to Him, He continually asked for something new.

Eventually the tailor was driven to desperation; he could think of nothing new, and to make matters worse, he was the only tailor in the whole Kingdom.

So he thought and he thought, and eventually hatched a plan — a really diabolical idea. He told the King that he had invented a new fabric which not only changed colors and shape into a new costume every moment, but that it would reveal those who were dimwitted, ignorant or stupid, or all three by a wonderful property...to a fool the fabric would appear invisible, and to the wise, it would appear ever-changing and stunningly beautiful.

"What terrific clothes," the King thought to Himself...of course to Himself — always to Himself, "just by wearing them I will be able to distinguish the wise from the fools."

The tailor was commissioned to fashion the new clothes at once. Weeks went by, and still the clothes did not arrive; and no wonder, because there was nothing to send. The tailor never intended to make anything, because he had run out of ideas and, through cunning, intended to deliver nothing whatever to the King, after a suitable period of time had elapsed to convince the King that the clothes were incredibly difficult to manufacture.

Finally the new suit of clothes was delivered to the King, and He excitedly opened the package, only to discover that He could see nothing at all...

But, not wishing to appear dimwitted, ignorant or stupid or all three, He pretended to dress Himself in the new clothes and went out among the people in His Kingdom.

And do you think for a moment that any of His subjects risked their heads by mentioning anything about his nudity?

Not on your life, they didn't!

Until a small child happened to say a little too loudly as the King passed by in procession, "Hey, look! The King is naked!"

A stunned silence passed through the crowd assembled there to witness the procession of the King and His ministers as the reverberations of the child's voice rippled across the square.

"just by wearing them I will be able to distinguish the wise from the fools."

"Now look at what you've done," the King wailed to the tailor. "Everyone thinks I'm a fool, going around naked."

"Nonsense, your Majesty," the tailor temporized. "Didn't they all see your ever-changing rainbow suit when you first emerged from the Palace? It's just the children who are unable to see it. Of course, they are ignorant. How could they know?

"I'll tell you what," he offered to the King, "I'll teach all the children to see your new clothes and, until they do, just ignore what they say about them."

The King thought this was a splendid plan, and the tailor was given the new job of teaching all the children to see His new clothes.

This went on for some time, but there was a flaw in the plan. In order to teach the children to see invisible — actually non-existent — clothes, and even to believe it in spite of their senses, very strong methods had to be employed.

These methods of hypnosis were so powerful that, as the children became immersed in the hallucination of the King's clothes, their vision of the real world dimmed and, by the time they reached adulthood, although they could now see the King's new clothes, they were unable to see the King Himself.

When the King complained to the tailor about this, the tailor replied, "Well, what do you want more? Do you want them to be able to see you or your new clothes? You can't have both, you know."

The King was very aware that the necessities of conditioning were such that vision was extremely altered from the real to the hallucinatory. He did not have to be reminded that it was impossible to have subjects able to see both Himself and His new clothes. Of course, He could have returned to wearing His old clothes but, compared to an ever-changing infinitely varied rainbow-colored costume, even if it did happen to be non-existent, they didn't seem at all adequate.

"Hey, look! The King is naked!"

"How does this sound?" the tailor inquired. "I'll still teach all the children to see the clothes, but I'll teach a few of your subjects — not the wise majority of the population, because they are needed to support the Kingdom, but the fools, those who are useless to the general purposes of life in any case — to see you. Of course, you must realize that when they learn to see you and not your clothes, you'll appear to them to be naked..." he added in a slightly apologetic tone.

"It's worth it," the King agreed. And so, some of the fools of the Kingdom — outsiders, misfits and those who, through some misfortune of nature were not content with hallucination — were taught to see the King.

And from that day to the present, the tailor has not been too awfully busy. And as for new ideas for new costumes for the King? Who needs aggravation?

The End

Commentary on the myth of *The King's New Klothes,* or; Why Do You Say He's Naked? He's Not Wearing Any Clothes!

G. was approached by a group of his students who had been working intensively on the puzzling question of why most people see the King's clothes but they do not see the naked King Himself even though His clothes are invisible or non-existent as described in the children's fairy tale *The King's New Klothes.*

G. indicated there are clues from analogous situations in the phenomenal world, like sub-atomic particles. He pointed out that although we cannot see atoms we can see their effects so we know they exist. In the same way, although most people cannot see the King they see His clothes and some know that He exists.

"One of the things one must do in order to work is see the King, tear your gaze from the clothes. One must realize, and it is a big step to realize this, that either the King is naked or, if He is wearing invisible clothes, He *appears* to be naked.

"We know the King is naked, so what do we know of the Queen? She would be the clothes. If all phenomena is the King's clothes, why do we see just her, and not the King?"

T. replied, "She catches our eye."

"If she is invisible, *how does she catch our eye?*"

"We are invisible too," D. answered.

"And the King is not invisible," said G. "What keeps your attention, your vision, rooted to the phenomenal? Is there anyway to see the King — to break through the veil of phenomena to see the King? Never mind why we would want to. Suffice it to say that in certain parts of work, it becomes necessary to see the King in all and everything.

"One cannot do this in ordinary ways, we can never come to it accidentally. The secret is safeguarded. Alone, one is unable to discover the exact method to see the King. Even with enough data, special help is necessary.

"The First Adam split into the Second Adam, plus Eve. Eve was tempted by Samael, who is also called Satan, in the Garden. How was a serpent able to seduce Eve?"

"Through sensing during the invocation of the Shekinah, who is the non-phenomenal part of Eve, and who remains in the Garden after the fall and expulsion from the Garden of the phenomenal part of Eve, you will discover that she is a serpent. You will know that the only one who sees Eve is Adam, her corresponding.

"Why, when Adam was seduced by his first wife, Lilith — a she-demon — were they not expelled from the Garden?

"Lilith was with the first Adam, Eve was with the Second Adam. Today, the children of Lilith are not serpents; Eve's children are serpents. If Eve was a serpent then all children of Eve were serpents."

"That is like the Jewish lineage," added J. "If the woman is Jewish, the children are Jewish. If the woman is a snake, the children are snakes."

G. continued, "If we are not snakes then we are not children of Eve."

"Who are we children of?" asked A.

"Lilith?" suggested L.

"That is one possibility, another is a demoness or fallen angel that cohabited with Adam..." said G. "Obviously we may have caught glimpses of the King, but we did not recognize the King. How would we recognize the King when we saw Him?

"In the Fourth Way we use a 'penetrating prayer' passed on from generation to generation, in the lineage of a school: taking only what we know about the situation as a starting point, to penetrate any unknown, any mystery..."

"The only thing that is real is the King; everything we are involved with is illusion — the King's clothes," said J.

"The clothes are the only part of the King which appears to exist," added F.

G. said, "We do not see the King, we see His clothes, and that is all we see. But we know the King is naked; the clothes are invisible or non-existent. We are looking at something invisible or non-existent and seeing something. Because we are seeing the invisible or non-existent, we cannot see the King.

"It is not that nothing exists; the King is really there, it is only His clothes that do not exist. It is just the phenomenal world that is the illusion.

"How is it that we can be brought to such a condition that we can see His clothes, but not the King Himself? How is it that we have come to this condition where we can see the invisible and not see the visible? What does this tell us about our perceptions?"

"That we do not see what is there, we see a reflection," said T.

"We see upside down," said A.

"We are seeing hallucinations," added J.

"We are seeing hallucinations, yes," G. responded. "Why? What is making us see hallucinations? If we know this, maybe we can stop having hallucinations.''

"Hypnotism," J. offered.

"Conditioning," suggested B.

"Yes," agreed G., "conditioning is a form of hypnosis. We must remember that some children immediately see the clothes, not the King; while some children immediately see the King, not the clothes. Why is this so?"

"Perhaps something happens at birth during the trip down the birth canal," suggested A.

"Nothing quite so complicated. You do not have the equipment to really know how to obtain the answer. Actually the answer is very simple, too obvious; always the purloined letter.

"There is a catalyst to all this, and the catalyst is usually of the same form in every kind of problem like this. We do not see the King right away. We can grind away our misperceptions little by little to penetrate the veil of hypnosis, if we continue to remember, no matter what we think we see, that the King is naked.

"This is the penetrating prayer: *No matter what I think I see, the King is naked.* Eventually we will see the King, although it may require many repetitions to see that it is true; to use this aid to vision in order to penetrate the phenomenal veil — the King's invisible clothes. It is sufficient to know what we are looking for, even though we do not yet see the King. All we need to know is that the King is naked."

"Would we recognize the King if we saw Him?" B. inquired.

"That is the next question," said G., "Would we recognize the King if we saw Him, or do we only recognize the Queen who envelops, blankets the King? The Queen is invisible, yet all we see is the Queen.

"The clothes are invisible, yet we see only the clothes. Can we tear our gaze from the clothes and put our gaze on the King, who is naked?

"We are hearing rumors of the existence of a great powerful Absolute Being living right in our midst, in front of our eyes, and yet we cannot see Him! Do you understand the irony of this? Do you know that all phenomenal events seem to support the visibility of the Queen?

"It is not just under special circumstances that the King is naked; the King is *always* naked. We can point to the King and say 'the King is not just naked now, He is *always* naked.'

"We see the King's clothes, but we do not see the King, but the King is naked. Is that a paradox? No, it is not. The King's clothes are invisible! Then why do I see the King's clothes, and not the King?

"There is not any easy way to see this. It requires use of the catalyst over a very long period of time; it requires *practice* to see the King.

"If you were an astronomer it would take a long time before you knew what you were looking at. Anyone can look at the stars but it takes *practice* to *see* the stars in a coherent formulation."

"Most people would not be able to do that alone although there are some who have done it," added J. "Someone must show you, there are very few people who can learn this by themselves."

"It requires perseverance and help," said G.

"There are books that show us what we are looking at," chimed in S.

"As I said," continued G. in a playfully severe tone, "it requires perseverance and help. So much for the help, now about the perseverance..."

After the group had stopped laughing, G. went on, "What do we know about the Shekinah and the Garden of Eden? The second Adam and Eve were expelled from the Garden of Eden. Remember that the Garden of Eden was as large as the whole universe, the whole world. That gives you a hint."

"That we are *in* the Garden of Eden?" questioned J.

"We are in exile from the garden — we see the King's clothes, not the King,"

Shekinah was not. She is wrapped around the Tree of Life, and she turns it into the tree of splendor. She glitters, turning it into a tree of a million rainbows. And she is left to guard the garden.

"It is forbidden to *study* the Kabala; it is not forbidden to *know* the Kabala. It is forbidden to study the Book of Zohar; yet it is not forbidden to know the Book of Zohar. It is not forbidden to *know* the Kabala. It is forbidden to *study* it. It is forbidden to study the Sephiroth, the Tree of Life; it is not forbidden to know the Sephiroth. It is forbidden to study the Law; it is not forbidden to know the Law.

"On the other hand, it is not forbidden to study the Shekinah in minute detail, or to know the Shekinah, in

No matter what I think I see, the King is naked.

replied G., "we have not gone anywhere; there is no where else to go. The Garden of Eden and the phenomenal world both appear in the same form.

"What do we know about the Garden of Eden? Are there any inhabitants? What do we know about the inhabitants of the Garden of Eden?

Suggested B., "We are still being seduced by the snake."

"Eve and Satan were definitely expelled from the garden," replied G., "so was Adam. Who was not? The

the biblical sense.

"In fact, the reuniting of the Shekinah, called the Bride of God, with the King is the entire task of the People of Israel.

"So it is forbidden to make data into intellectual knowledge," stated J.

"We have data," said G., "but can never put it together in the right way without help. We must know how before we can do. Before we get data we must have something in which the data can take root.

"After a long time we begin to

understand that what we see is not really what it appears to be. We begin, after a long time, to really see that the King is naked.

"Why is the King wearing the Queen as clothes? Why? We hear rumors that the Queen is the ultimate accommodator. Of course she is; she is invisible. Do you understand what that means?

"I will show you the ultimate card trick, but I will need invisible playing cards..."

G. asked J. to name a card, and then he would show her the invisible card. G. continued, "I can do this indefinitely with invisible cards. If you really began to *see* the cards after a while..." The group burst into laughter at the absurdity of this idea, and then stopped laughing when he added, "that would correspond more or less to your present conditioning now.

"The King is right here; we are a hair's breadth away from the Garden of Eden. Why can we not see the Garden of Eden?"

"We do not know how to look for it?" guessed L.

"You know now how to look for the King," replied G., "Why not look for the garden the same way? We are one hair's breadth from the Kingdom of Heaven, a hair's breadth from the Garden of Eden, a hair's breadth from the Eternal World. We are *in* it, yet *not* in it. We are liberated, yet we do not know it."

"As Mephistopheles said on the occasion of his conjuration by the good Doctor Faustus, 'Why, Faustus, this *is* Hell, *nor am I out of it.* Of all the inhabitants of Hell, none but Lucifer Knows that Hell *is* Hell'."

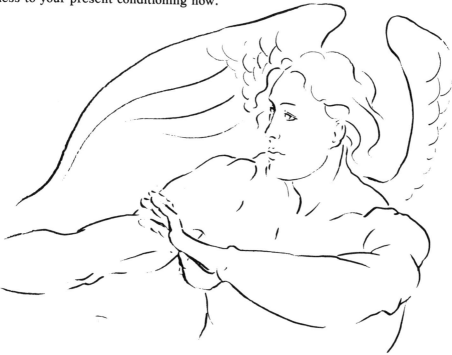

The Symptoms of Death

If you're about to die or you've taken a drug, you'll begin to notice several terrifying sensations and cosmic revelations as the phenomenal veil is ripped away, revealing for the first time since the last time you passed away from the organic world, the endless, eternal unveiled kingdom of the void.

At the same time, you'll experience a mind-numbing personal cataclysm as you're hurtled at twice the speed of light into a dark and unknown world in which everything seems almost the same as it was before, only more so.

Don't worry about those strange new sensations and cosmic thoughts. They're not important. After all, you're dead! What *more* can happen? After you've taken rebirth you'll be able to look back on all this and laugh.

These sensations are useful for anticipating your exact moment of passage and, if you've been practicing at our popular intensives and workshops, you can use these sensations to automatically produce, by organically reinforced association, a series of psychological, emotional and instinctive mechanisms which maintain a sense of balance, however false, during the total loss of memory, vision, hearing, sensation and personal identity during the passage through the portal of death, through which you're inevitably dragged just as you're getting the hang of organic life.

Identity, environment, memory —

they'll all go out the window, but who needs that junk, anyway?

It's so easy to just expel your last breath out in a sigh of relief and fall face-first into your plate of spaghetti and meatballs in total surrender to the usual Perfect, Shining, Endless Void without objects, states of consciousness, identity, time, space, filled parking lots and empty weekends you've been struggling to hold onto. When you finally give up the effort of maintaining your organic-headbrain personal identity, you'll understand the mystique of peanut butter by the spoonful.

As the veil is lifted, you'll feel several sensations grouped together as a series of symptoms, the first of which is a sensation of heavy pressure, like melting into an all-wool union-suit while wearing a pair of lead boots, will descend on you all of a sudden.

Don't worry about this sensation; you've probably got a good fifteen minutes to an hour and a half left to handle any last-minute details, and, if you have a friend visiting you at your deathbed, and your friend is so inclined, you still have time for a wonderfully refreshing foot massage.

The second sensation will be a clammy coldness alternating with the sweats, as if your body is burning up. This is just one symptom of hypothermia, in which the body's heat is reduced. Hey, nothing to worry about . . . passage is still *minutes* away!

The third sensation is a definite feeling that your body is about to explode. You may actually get the sensation of being blown into smithereens and dispersed by the wind. *Now* you have something to *worry* about! Passage is only moments away. Try to relax and think of something pleasant.

The fourth sensation isn't really a sensation — it's a total lack of sensations. Suddenly, although your mind has miraculously opened up, offering a breathtaking and profound view of the entire Creation, it doesn't *refer* to anything. This vision plus fifty cents will get you a one-way ride on a city bus.

In addition to these sensations, there may be other noticeable sensations or psychological events, interludes, fugues, schisms or other minor disorders which occur prior to passage from the organic world to Wherever You're Going...

There might be loss of control over facial muscles, causing an insipid smile or that unoccupied look usually reserved for high school seniors.

You might periodically lose your hearing, or words and phrases which made sense before might not make the same sense they made before when you understood what they were saying by the words and phrases they might be understood and made sense before when you understood what they meant by what they said.

There might be loss of sight or radical changes in vision vision vision.

Your breath might be ragged, particularly if you're getting more than just a foot massage.

You might find yourself shivering or sweating, and you might have an uncontrollable desire to remove your clothes and walk around. Unless you're expected to recover, this might be a good idea. Who knows what last-minute adventures might be in store for you?

You may feel a lethargic calm descend over you. If you've spent your life as a lawyer or on a graduate fellowship, or dropped lethargic acid with the hippies in the Haight-Ashbury District of San Francisco, you might not notice this.

There may be a loss of attention caused by falling over unconscious on the floor.

You may notice that your breathing has mysteriously stopped several minutes ago and that you can't move your limbs. In this case, don't bother trying to talk.

When all these symptoms of approaching death have been completed, the reader should gently recite into the voyager's ear in a low tone of voice: "So long, sucker, you're on your own."

After *ALL* you're

First Stage
The Moment of Death

When the Clear Light overwhelms the senses, opening the vision to the Eternal World, anyone who has bought this book — unless they got it on a discount rack or in a Remaindered Bin — will immediately obtain liberation from the Realm of the Folding Lotus — a polite euphemism for the Eternal Creation — into the Realm of the Clear Light, in which they will be ushered into the presence of the Invisible and Silent Buddha or given the point-spreads of all the national league games of the next decade and sent back to earth with a hundred dollars and a new suit of clothes.

We're assuming that you have attained the power to die voluntarily without clutching and clinging to the body, and...and...and that you've developed the ability to recog-

Identity, environment, memory —

can blend with the Clear Light, moving directly from the dream state of organic life into the expanded state of total diffusion in the endless crystal waters of the Clear Light without passing Go and without collecting two hundred...hey! You're drifting. Pay attention, okay?

You'll feel the shades of emotion blending into the background as you, the dreamer, blend directly into Reality by diffusion with the patchwork quilt, which is reality without dimension, the unveiled vision of the Creation, about which I'll explain sometime later on if I have time. Get it? Time...little continuum joke.

If possible, the teacher from whom you received your initiation during organic life should attend, but knowing these guys, he probably won't, so someone who knows him or works with him or who has read at least one of his books should be there, and if that isn't possible, then anyone who can read clearly and distinctly and doesn't sound like he has potatoes in his mouth should read these instructions

they'll all go out the window, but who needs that JUNK anyway?

nize the vision of the King when He reveals Himself and His Kingdom, mad flasher that He is, so that at the moment of separation from the organic body you

as often as possible before your body dies so you can establish some connection with his or her voice and get a foot massage.

3

No matter who comes to read for you, try to play on their sympathy so you can get a foot massage at least once a day. You know, "before I...go...could you...massage my...I don't want to ask you to do any more than you're already doing, but...could you massage my...my..." and so forth. This is good therapy for the reader as well.

If you feel like sleeping during the moments of impending passage — a polite euphemism for wearing a wooden kimono, — I don't care what the Tibetan Buddhists say, I say, go ahead and sleep. You don't want to be exhausted after you die.

Supposedly the Clear Light is the most critical and vital period of passage. Big deal. If you want to sleep, the least they can do is let you sleep. All Sentient Beings experience the Clear Light at this point, but if you haven't concerned yourself about it before, why worry about it now?

The exact duration of the Clear Light state depends on the condition of the nervous system, organs and circulatory system; it particularly depends on whether or not you have abdominal gas at the time of departure.

If you happen to have experience in the esoteric practices of *Qua-Si-Mo-Do* or *Thung-Ka-Po*, which, as everybody knows, require years and years of serious efforts fourteen to eighteen hours a day, you're in luck, because with that kind of training you should be able to easily maintain the Clear Light State and make it last for several days, during which you'll have plenty of time to attain Liberation in the highest realm outside Creation.

If not, you'll just have to suffer like any other sucker when you get your face rearranged during the Third Stage just prior to rebirth.

There is a remedy for this, however, and it isn't necessary to prepare for years

die voluntarily without clutching to the BODY clinging and • • • and • • • and • • •

The interval between the final in-breath and the final outbreath is the time when the vital force remains in the Median Nerve, but since nobody knows exactly which nerve that is, it's just another distracting fact to clutter up the situation, as far as I'm concerned.

and years, as in the case of the two esoteric practices previously mentioned.

If you happen to have included a codicil in your last will and testament bequeathing a large proportion of your estate to the nonprofit tax-exempt organization founded by the author of this book, *something can be arranged.*

Only a highly trained spiritual adept or someone who had left their estate in the right hands would be able to pass directly from the organic world into the diffused voidness outside Creation without diving head-first into rebirth as a coolie in some Southeast-Asian rice paddy.

something CAN be arranged.

Just as an infant learns how to operate in the organic world, a voyager set adrift in the unveiled vision of the Diffused State quickly learns how to crawl, walk, talk and use the potty under the unusual conditions encountered between organic incarnations.

millionth time.

The spirit body with which you'll be passing through the Eternal World is an exact duplicate of the organic body you had while you were on earth, with the exception of the memory, personality, clothes, and dental work, excluding periodontal care.

The psychic nervous system is an exact counterpart of the organic nervous system, and resonates with it during the passage through the moment of death and for several hours afterward, unless you have ordered a psychic karma-ectomy by mail from our direct-sales department in California, for a nominal donation.

After passing from the phenomenal-organic world, you'll hear the reader — and I should mention now that readers are available on a living-trust or pre-need payment plan — continue reading the Clear Light instructions somewhere near the recently occupied cadaver, until a yellow pus begins to ooze out of the various apertures of the body, after which your former organic body is something

Jammed down a birth canal for the ten-millionth time.

Naturally, it is better to gain this experience at one of our weekend workshops than to try to achieve liberation, awakening, rebirth in a higher world or what-have-you while you're being jammed down a birth canal for the ten-

only a mortician could love.

The reader will then hang a "vacancy" sign on the bedpost, and continue reading in a less aesthetically discommoding atmosphere.

5

Confronting the Clear Light

If the reader is sincerely and genuinely interested in making serious efforts to produce the liberation of the voyager during the passage from death to rebirth — and an endowment or a bequest is certainly good insurance toward this end — the stripped consciousness which passes from organic life into the Eternal World will without a doubt completely penetrate the hallucination of phenomenal visions, wisely taking root in the Clear Light in which endless reruns of *Star-Trek*, *Gilligan's Island* and *Mash* flow more or less continuously, interspersed with reruns of the voyager's own spectacular exploits among the primitive savages of the phenomenal world.

If the voyager recognizes the phenomenal world as the crystallized form of the Creation, the vision of Minnie Mouse in sexual union with Goofy could just by itself cause spontaneous liberation.

See you next time **around!**

If you stop to think about it, that would save a lot of time. The voyager wouldn't have to pass through all those strange visions and whatnot in all those halls and chambers during the unravelling of consciousness which occurs in the Second Stage and sometimes in the First Stage, depending upon the strength, purity and quality of whatever it is you happen to be on at the moment.

Qua-Si-Mo-Do Thung-Ka-Po

At this point you should be experiencing the Clear Light, but should you happen to notice that nothing is happening or has ever happened or ever will happen — and especially if you see a blinking sign that reads "!NO FUMAR!" it will help you in this case to remember that your present consciousness is in reality unformed and void, having been cancelled a long time ago by a failure to make regular payments.

Your real nature is the same as if the Clear Light itself. You really are the Clear Light and at the same time you're the mirror which reflects the Clear Light.

As a matter of fact, you are also the reflection of the Clear Light reflected in the mirror which reflects the endless ocean of Clear Light and is made of Clear Light, which information I happen to have obtained directly from a voice in an empty room with invisible walls.

You might be tempted at this moment to ask, of nobody in particular, ''Hey, where did everybody go?''. Don't worry about this impulse; it's perfectly normal to ask a question like that when you find yourself suspended in nothingness, surrounded by absolute zero. Hearing an answer, however... Now, *that* isn't normal.

And so the First Clear Light is recognized and spontaneous liberation from the Creation is achieved. Feels great, doesn't it? I knew you'd be pleased.

But just in case something has gone wrong — a thousand-to-one long-shot, I admit, but possible nevertheless — perhaps we'd better continue these instructions.

as a COOLIE in some Southeast-Asian ricepaddy

Second Clear Light

We can assume that there has been no terrific blinding flash of recognition. Never mind; no big deal. It's becoming obvious that, for you, the clarified nonphenomenal vision did not open to new and awesome vistas of knowledge and insight. It's not unusual. This sort of thing happens occasionally, especially to someone very low on the spiritual totem pole.

Evidently the dawning of Absolute Truth made little or no impression on you, and the diffusion of consciousness and the endless endlessness of the infinite shining void produced only the most vague effect on your feelings of inadequacy and personal insecurity... little emotional leftovers from yesterday's lunch... since you can still hear and understand my instructions. Otherwise you'd be well on your way to complete

seldom mistaken in cases like yours... I've seen them come and I've seen them go — you should now be able to see the vision of the Second Clear Light before you, on both sides of you, above you, below you, and — if you're paying really close attention — behind you.

It's been about an hour since you were yanked unceremoniously out of the phenomenal world, and the vital force ought to have flowed out of the organic nervous system channels and dribbled their way into the Eternal World along with your sense of presence, however vague it may be at this stage of the game.

A lucid state should have overwhelmed you not more than a few minutes ago, causing ecstasy and a state of high indifference.

If this has not occurred and does not occur within a very short time, it means that all your earlier feelings of inadequacy and insecurity were fully justified and you belong, as you thought all along, on the lower end of the spiritual totem pole, which is where you are.

get a foot massage...
get a foot massage...
could you massage...my...my...

and permanent liberation, in which case, you wouldn't be able to hear and understand my instructions.

If I'm right about this — and I'm

This Second Clear Light will be less intense than the First Clear Light, unless something has gone wrong. Gone wrong. Gone wrong... And why should everything all of a sudden go right?

On the first pass through the Clear Light, the consciousness of presence reaches the highest level of sensation as it encounters the pure Life-Force, but on the second bounce, the energy is lower and so, a much lower peak is achieved.

lower and more organic as the escape velocity from your recent passage out of the phenomenal world begins to pass wind.

Finally, when this escape-force has been fully spent in futile efforts to achieve some imaginary Eternal Static

when *He* reveals *Himself* and *His Kingdom,* mad flasher that *He* is

But if you went to sleep alive last night and woke up dead this morning, it won't make much difference, will it?

On the other hand, if you're on something, you'll probably want to drop another two hundred and fifty micrograms, unless you're on something else, in which case you may decide to drop another two-hundred milligram cap.

This would be a serious error, because in another few moments a secondary wave will break, and you wouldn't want to try to force your guts, which are presently trying to adjust to having moments ago dissolved in a puddle of goo on the floor, to digest a gelatin capsule in the middle of a peak, even a secondary peak.

The waves of sensation may feel stronger and have a cumulative effect, but these secondary peaks are actually lower than the first, and they'll get even

State of Unending Pleasure and Total Absence of Pain, you'll undoubtedly be drawn inexorably downward into the worst possible rebirth as a South American politician, unless you meditate on the Guru.

Don't be distracted. Concentrate on the Guru. Meditate on the Guru as if he were the reflection of the moon upon the water, the reflection of your own Guru-nature. And stop asking, "What's a Guru?", because nobody else knows, either.

Even those who would not ordinarily expect to recognize the Clear Light without help, if they meditate on the Guru, are almost certain to obtain liberation in the Clear Light, whatever *that* means.

Someone who, while living in the organic world currently called earth, has learned to recognize the Guru, will certainly be able to recognize the Guru in the Eternal World, even if he is unfamiliar with the Clear Light. Such a voyager is easily impressed.

If you only know the theory but not the practice of this teaching, you may become bewildered and confused, or bewildered *or* confused, or bewildered but *not* confused, or confused but not *bewildered* by this experience or not, as the case may be in your case as opposed to other cases which, because they are not entirely unique, will certainly be different from yours barring coincidences of events and the unfolding of the perpetual lotus.

you are unable to handle the sensations and visions of the Eternal World beyond the Veil, you now know what they — meaning various Eastern saints and sages — were referring to when they warned you about *karma*.

You may grow so confused by the unexpected changes in this world beyond the Veil that you automatically spiral downward into rebirth as a 9 to 5 working stiff, just because it's the only stable reality with which you are familiar.

Even one who is highly skilled in the between-lives state may, through inattention, fear or repulsion, try to squirm

Time . . . . *continuum*
Time . . . . *continuum*
Time . . . . *continuum*
Get it? Time . . . *little continuum* J
Time . . . . *continuum*
Time . . . . *continuum*
Time . . . . *continuum*

Untrained voyagers who have been profoundly immersed in the ordinary parade of events in daily life to the exclusion of the strange and unusual visions of the Eternal Kingdom should be back at work in a day or two without losing vacation time or dipping too deeply into workmen's compensation benefits.

If you have been identified with the events of ordinary life to the extent that

out of the sensations that occur during passage through the Eternal World, thereby inexorably taking an involuntary dump, leading to yet another organic rebirth.

In still another case, you may have become familiar with the visions and sensations of the Clear Light and yet, because of a particularly grim and horrible accident which was the immediate cause of your passage from the organic world and about which you don't want to talk just yet, you were thrown so badly out of whack that you were just plain unable to recover your equilibrium without help.

That's why this book is here now. Too bad you're not . . .

Also, there may be voyagers who — although they are familiar with this teaching — have fallen into various forms of degraded behavior . . . passions, wild parties, X-rated videotapes and furtive visits to local massage parlors . . . in which case, these instructions from this book are extremely vital and a larger bequest or endowment to the nonprofit organization founded by the author is clearly indicated.

While in the Second Clear Light, one forms what is called the Radiant Body of Light. Nobody knows why it's called that, or who decided to name it, but if you could see it in a mirror, you'd agree that that's what it looks like.

Not realizing that you've passed from the organic world, you might wonder about the sudden clarity which has descended over you, unless you've had prior experience as a resident in the mildly-disturbed ward or had a four-by-twelve rafter or a floor-joist land square on your frontal occipital once or twice.

You might feel a sudden compulsion to wander aimlessly but urgently, or to perform the habitual functions you performed during your brief sojourn on the planet Earth, but this is a very good time to relax and take stock of the situation.

The inexorable karmic visions which are the result of the reversal of organic consciousness in an inexorable unwinding process, have not yet begun, and so, luckily, you have a few more moments in the calm before the storm, before all hell lets loose.

bewildered AND
confused, OR
bewildered OR *OR*
confused, OR
bewildered OR BUT *NOT*
confused, OR
confused' BUT NOT
bewildered.

Unfortunately, no voyager I've ever heard of has had any idea how to use these few moments of calm to any advantage.

The Clear Light — even the Secondary Clear Light, comparatively weak as it is — has the effect of dispersing the negative effects of organic conditioning, just as the sun's radiations dispel the darkness, and as some people who don't use deodorant are able to dispel a gathering of Methodists.

The passage through the First Clear Light generally awakens the Body of Light and calls attention to the endlessness of it all, while the Secondary Clear Light awakens the state of clarity, in which you will suddenly be able to understand everything you didn't understand before.

11

If for some reason you aren't able to understand anything, don't panic. It just means that the Secondary Radiation didn't awaken the state of clarity, which means that in about fifteen trillion years you'll slam back into rebirth, barring some miracle or other which, by the way,

and waking more and more ... And three ... fully awake now, feeling just fine.

Congratulations. You have achieved total liberation forever from the Creation and from all karmic visions and hallucinations.

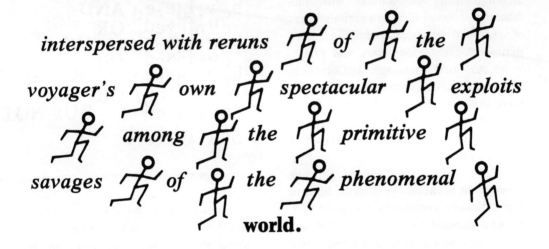

interspersed with reruns of the voyager's own spectacular exploits among the primitive savages of the **phenomenal world.**

can be arranged for a small fee, amounting to just an honorarium, really.

At this time you ought to be able to penetrate beyond the illusion of who you were in the organic world to who you really are in the eternal world.

Listen, you do that, and you'll never be troubled by organic karmic phenomenal visions again or by the backward unravelling of a life that never really happened, and wouldn't have mattered if it had, but didn't.

On the count of three, you will awaken fully and completely. One ... more and more awake ... Two, feeling wonderful

But ... I can't help worrying ... just in case you missed a *chakra* somewhere on the way toward liberation ... it might be wise to continue these instructions ...

Meditate on the Guru ...
and stop asking,
"What's a Guru",
because nobody else
knows, either.

Second Stage
First Karmic Visions

This is the part nobody likes, when the visions begin their slow unwinding process, reversing your exposure to the organic timestream in the midst of Creation.

Some of these visions may seem strange if you haven't penetrated beyond the veil separating the conscious from the unconscious mind during your stay at Hotel Organic Life on the planet Earth.

If you're worried about attaining spontaneous liberation now during the hallucinatory visions just because you missed getting off the train during your passage through the First, Second and Third Clear Light radiations, don't worry...it's still vaguely possible to get out of this whirling pool of confusion before you're thrust back into the uterus of Our Lady of Perpetual Boredom by the forces of karma and gastro-intestinal necessity and ordered to report for tailbrain duty in a newborn brontosaurus.

When the strange visions and sensations begin, it's very important to pay attention to these instructions if you can, so you don't fall into the sensations and follow them down into one or another of the lower worlds from which you might not be able to escape for a long time.

On the other hand, these visions *do* tend to grab the attention by the balls and keep it rooted, you should pardon the expression, to the spot, don't they? So do what you can at this point to keep your attention sharpened and alert, so you'll be able to follow what I'm trying to tell you, especially if the words don't make any sense whatever, in which case, if you don't understand what I'm saying right now, you won't have understood anything I've said so far, including what I'm saying now, in which case you probably have no idea what I'm saying. Are you following this line of reasoning?

At about this time, if you were recently human, you'll see the body being stripped of its clothes. If you were another kind of animal, especially of the endangered species variety, you'll be helplessly watching somebody skinning your beautiful hide to grace some lovely lady's wardrobe in Beverly Hills.

The food offerings will be set aside or eaten by the priests if you were an Egyptian, a Tibetan, or an American Yogi.

If you were Irish, the food offerings will be set aside and forgotten entirely in favor of the 86 proof whiskey, and your body will be stuffed and mounted so they can keep the party going.

If you were Jewish, the food offerings will be crammed down the throat disregarding whether the body is alive or dead, what you don't eat will be put aside for later, and a piece of fruit will be placed in your rigor-mortised hand so you shouldn't go hungry later.

The body will then, if things go according to custom, be gently covered by a linen shroud or shoved headfirst into an oversize black plastic garbage baggie and dumped into a black pickup truck to be transported to the mortuary, about which we'll go into some detail later on, perhaps after you've taken rebirth again, when you have the stomach for it.

Then the bedroom or shared or private room — unless you were a charity case in a common ward or your body died out in the woods someplace and decomposed before somebody could claim it and bill the survivors for the funeral expenses — would be swept and mopped, and your bad vibes and disease scrubbed out of existence by a standard hospital-strength antiseptic solution.

Just at that moment, you will undoubtedly experience various disturbing sounds besides those of uncle Albert and aunt Martha. The light will seem very, very strange.

Objects may appear to be illuminated from within themselves rather than from an outside source, and strange sensations or emotions may pass through you, producing the effect of having been pierced by intense radiation during a nuclear mishap.

Don't forget this vital secret. Underline it in the book.

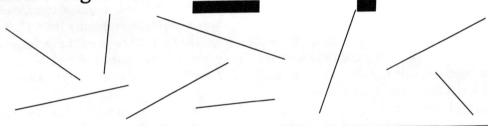

After the body has been placed on view, the inevitable friends and relatives will wander aimlessly through the slumber room at the mortuary making the equally inevitable weeping sounds, dumping flowers with large gift cards on them telling you who bought flowers and who didn't, wearing corsages, white carnations and the customary expressions of grief, muttering something about how well you looked just before you died.

Can't you just hear aunt Martha telling uncle Albert, "What a nice tan! He never had a nice tan like that when he was alive! That trip to Florida did him a *world* of good!"

Don't allow these sounds, visions, sensations or emotions, no matter how awesome, **disgusting** or inconvenient, to discommode you for a moment. Just have some more tea and relax until it passes, and it will, before you can say 'Jiminy Cricket'. As a matter of fact, if you're on the right stuff, a lot of things can happen before you're able to say anything at all, even 'yike!' or 'shit, what was *that?*'

Fatigue and emotional exhaustion can cause unpleasant reactions to these otherwise harmless little nonphenomenal pranks.

You will experience three main stages of visions in your passage through the eternal world from the time you leave the organic world until you return to it or to something worse.

> ## " What a nice tan! He never had a nice tan like that when he was alive! "

The first is the moment of death and the dawning of the Clear Light. You had that three times already, and look at you. You ought to be ashamed of yourself, spiraling down like this. Just wait till your Father gets home! Listen, there he is now! Oh, boy, are you going to get it!

See? The karmic visions are happening already. I *told* you Something Like This Was Going To Happen, but no, you wouldn't listen. Now you'll probably blame me, but is it *my* fault you don't listen? Is it *my* fault you don't pay attention? Why can't you be like Buddha or one of those saints? Why don't you get a job and *work* for a living instead of hanging around dead?

Never mind, someday you'll learn. Meanwhile, while we're talking, the second stage in the unravelling of the karmic visions producing the illusion of passage through time and space which you call ''life'' has already begun.

These visions will occur in more or less reverse sequence from the way you experienced them during your stay on Earth, but they'll carry the same persuasive force and influence you to react to them as if they're really happening to you, unless you remember that they're only imaginary visions and that they can't grab you and make you do strange things, unusual things, bizarre things, fun things, *unless you allow them to.*

The third stage is the re-formation of your identity into something like what you had before, unless you need something else for your evolution and can keep your attention alert until you're about to enter rebirth. Now you should be prepared to enter the second stage in which the karmic visions unfold before your very eyes, so to speak.

Try to remember where you are, and concentrate your attention on these instructions, or you may be swept up by the power of these visions and sensations and flushed down the toilet of automatic rebirth.

> ## 'Jiminy Cricket' • • •
> ## 'yike!' • • •
> ## 'shit' • • •
> what was *that?*

''That trip to Florida did him a

world

of good!''

15

Concentrate your attention and repeat with me:

"I'm not the only one who ever left the organic world. Lots of others have done it too. It's not as if they can't do *without* me. There are *plenty* of others who could easily take my place . . .

"Besides, I won't be gone *that* long. What's the big deal? Why work your butt off, slaving over some hot body year after year, if you can't get a couple of days off now and then?

"I won't cling to the habits of the organic world . . . except for that one harmless little habit . . . no, never mind . . . not even that one little habit, no matter how insignificant and harmless it may seem to me now.

"I won't wander around steeped in organic dreams in this or any other world. I'll remember where I am, and who I really am. I'm not going to let the sensations weird me out. I wish these bizarre sensations to be used for the invocation of the presence of my presence into the present . . . whatever *that* means!

"Gee, I feel better now. Maybe I should blow it more often . . ."

By now, you should remember who you really are, but just in case you don't, write it down on a piece of paper if you happen to have a pen or pencil handy.

When the terror of uncertainty overtakes you here, with every thought of fear, terror, awe or boredom set aside, try to recognize the unravelling karmic visions which held you in their spell and don't become lost in them, identified with them, caught up in their fascinating rhythm, driving you wild . . .

Don't believe in their reality. You have to see the visions and sense the sensations, but nothing in the book says you have to believe in their reality.

At this all-important liberating moment, this golden opportunity, try to flow with these waves of blissful and horrible visions, these stunningly beautiful and monstrous hordes of thoughts, visions, emotions and sensations arising from your own central source of organic hallucination.

Now you can see these visions for what they are. Blissful and horrible as they may seem, they are completely without influence over you. They have no power to make you do or say anything, as long as you remember that they are just the products of your own source of visions.

> # I wish these bizarre sensations to be used for the invocation of the presence of my presence into the present . . . whatever *that* means!

Don't forget this vital secret. Underline it in the book so you can find it any time you need to remember it, unless, of course, you forget where you put the book or what the underline means.

If you're afraid you might lose the book, just carve a copy on an ivory slab or copy the key passages on pure lamb parchment and put it in the secret compartment in your wallet or purse.

flushed down the toilet of automatic re BIRTH

If you have trouble locating lamb parchment, I'd like to mention now that our bookstore, which services most of the known world, carries lamb parchment at extremely reasonable prices and, as a matter of fact, also stocks a complete line of terminal midwifery supplies including candles, incenses and oils.

Order blanks for supplies are in the back of the book. If they've all been used, just write to the catalog department in California.

Now listen, and listen Good! When you involuntarily left the organic world, you must have glimpsed, at least momentarily, the Absolute Truth, such as it is, because you had to pass through it on your way out.

You couldn't miss it . . . subtle, dazzling, brilliant, awesome.

Doesn't ring a bell? Never mind, forget I even mentioned it. Let's get on with the instructions for the Second Stage and hope for a break in the clouds sooner or later, before you're thrown unceremoniously into the first fertile egg that comes along.

Can you see a continuous stream of vibrating, mirror-like radiation moving across the endless landscape, slightly to your left?

If you listen very carefully, you'll notice that, from the midst of that radiation will emerge the natural sounds of the Eternal World rumbling and reverberating like the sound of the Paramus New Jersey Marching Band. Don't

be afraid of that sound, and don't be attracted to it either, not to the extent of buying season tickets.

That sound is the natural sound of your own Being. It is your own sound, the sound of *you*. This deep, reverberating, rumbling sound comes and goes in waves, depending on what you ate the night before you died.

Since you no longer have an organic body, whatever happens can't hurt you, whether it's a sensation, a vision, a sound or a radiation, so you can feel free to just allow events to pass through you like getting down off a duck.

Look at it this way . . . how can they make you any more dead than you are at this very moment?

It should be enough just to know that these visions and sensations are your own visions, produced by your own source of visions and sensations.

how can they make you any more dea... than you are at this very moment?

It *should* be enough, but why should things all of a sudden be different with you than they have been for the past seven hundred trillion years?

Just hearing these ideas won't help you, O nobly unborn, unless you are able to concentrate your presence and attention and focus on what I'm saying to you!

Don't allow your attention to be distracted. If you don't recognize these visions and sensations as the reverberations of your organic life, and if you haven't prepared thoroughly for this experience during your life on earth, boy, are *you* in for a shock!

If the lightshow doesn't overwhelm you, the sounds from the stack speakers and overhead PA system cause total confusion, or the sensations caused by compulsive urges to rock out fill you with terror and fear, or the awesome tubular emotions don't drive you right into rebirth, the sight of the Naked King certainly will!

the sound of
YOU
• • • deep
• • • reverberating
• • • rumbling
• • • in waves

depending on what you ate the night before you died.

Hey, the Vision of the Naked King has been enough to drive the most hardened yogi completely off his rocker.

SEE?

The karmic visions are happening already.

The Peaceful Guides

Assuming that you'll be compelled to pass through the whole spectrum of visions in the second stage as most voyagers are, I'll explain in full detail what the problems and dangers are of each vision.

You've been in a dead faint, so to speak, and missed the best part, but never mind; by now you've fully recovered, not that it matters anymore.

The visions you're about to see, the emotions you're about to feel, and the sensations you're about to sense, are caused by the unwinding of your organic consciousness and the trailers for next week's coming attractions.

As you've no doubt noticed, the Six Sweet Worlds of Organic Creation are rising in a swirling uproar all around you.

As your identity crumbles into its five basic component parts, you'll be left with no time to think of a way out of this and nothing to think with anyway.

But don't worry. You'll be carried along like a log in water, and soon enough you'll be back in the saddle again.

You couldn't MISS ^{it} • • • SUBtle,
DAZZling,
BRILLiant,
ALL^{some.}

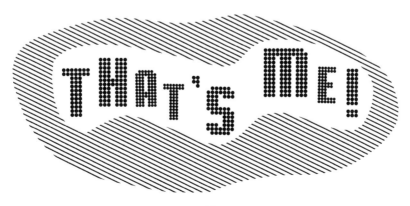

ITEM

The Patchwork Quilt

G. asked, "Does anyone know of the crazy patchwork quilt?"

"The mantle of the dervish," J. suggested.

"Have you heard of quilting bees? Women sit in a circle making quilts. Where? Not in a barn or kitchen, but in church. Each lady would bring her patches to be added to the quilt. It was a community gathering.

"The patchwork mantle of a dervish, his robe, is a picture of God. This," G. paused sweeping his hand across to indicate the entire room and its contents, "is also a patchwork quilt, a picture of God. You will understand eventually; someday you may penetrate the patchwork with your vision and see God.

"The patchwork quilt was also a community project in the Middle East. The story of Joseph and his robe is a story from antiquity, from Biblical times, well known in the Middle East because of the allegory involved. Joseph's Robe of Many Colors was a patchwork quilt. The story reminded people to see God by viewing the blended form of the quilt as a whole thing-in-itself."

"G., you said earlier that we pass into the phenomenal world by imposing phenomena on the nonphenomenal world; is this right?" M. asked.

"Yes, that is right," G. said. "I can prove it to you. Where are you right now?"

"In a room," M. replied.

"You are in fact," G. clarified, "in the nonphenomenal world; but you do not know it. You are a hair's breadth from the Garden of Eden.

"We do not know, because we impose phenomenal habits, reactions, forms, and limits on the nonphenomenal world. When we are able to stop ourselves from habitually imposing phenomenal separation of forms on the nonphenomenal world, we pass directly into the nonphenomenal world. If we impose the phenomenal world on the nonphenomenal we either take rebirth or throw ourselves into a second-stage deterioration which also leads eventually to rebirth. In other words, we respond to the nonphenomenal with phenomenal reactions. Almost certainly this will occur within the first few minutes of exposure to the nonphenomenal world without the automatic buffer of phenomena.

"Does anyone know what a yantra is? A yantra is a visual meditation device. Imagine sitting before an abstract painting for several years. Eventually one will talk to it, and it will talk to you. One will see forms, hallucinations. What we are seeing right now is not three-dimensional. We are looking into a hollow sphere in which there are blotches of color and shape which suggest forms. After a while sheer *ennui* suggests movement and forms, then finally, significance.

"Imagine a hollow sphere made of a mirror, producing a total reflection. Now imagine that on the inside of the sphere are painted many fuzzy indistinct forms. Where the eyes on these figures would be, imagine just holes.

"Next, imagine an organism sufficiently large to cover, like a thin film, the entire sphere from the outside, which brings each of its myriad eyes to where each of the holes are in the sphere.

"Everything we see from one peripheral point to the other and from top to bottom is what we want to see. It is our subjective vision. If it did not seduce us into involvement then it would involve us through fear, sensation, passion or something else which would make us wish to become involved.

"When we can see both the phenomenal and nonphenomenal worlds voluntarily, we have achieved a certain balance, after which we can learn to work. Our viewpoint on what happens to us is very different after we have seen the angelic world and understood what we have seen. On our voluntary return to the phenomenal, we are able to understand the forces which move us, and perhaps take a more voluntary part in the wonderful cosmic dance of which we are each a vital part."

21

First Vision

The chamber you seem to be in now will begin to glow with a dim violet radiation...Too bad you don't have a few blacklight posters, huh?

This violet radiation is the source of what we call "space". You're looking directly at *matter* resolved into its most primal form, even more primal than a Dior original!

In just a moment or two, you should notice a sensation as if radiation just penetrated your body. Nothing to worry about, just radiation penetrating your body.

This radiation burns away karma, which is the mysterious force that makes you do what you do if you allow it to.

Of course, if you try to resist the radiation, it will penetrate you anyway, but in that case, because you resisted, it won't do you any good.

thoughts.

Just relax and let the radiation do its work. Try to think of something pleasant if you can remember anything pleasant at this point. One thing that might cheer you up is that there is no judgment, no punishment, no reward...just overwhelming love.

But if you just can't relax, don't panic. Try to remain very, very still. If you happen to be breathing, that's all right — just residual organic habit. The craving for oxygen will pass eventually, if you don't reinforce it by whimpering with fear.

You've doubtless noticed by now a soft, perhaps somewhat sinister white light from which a peculiar sensation of peaceful lethargy seems to emanate.

This is the light of the Angelic World and, although it might appear less threatening than the alternatives, perhaps even pleasant in comparison, if you allow yourself to get dragged into it, you'll be forced to wander around as an angel through all six worlds before you find your way back out again. You know how it is...one drink leads to another.

Don't pay any attention to the soft,

The reader will then hang a **VACANCY** sign on the bedpost.

Might as well allow it to dissolve your karma, your sense of ego, and your habitual tendencies, actions and

seductive sensation of the white light. Ignore it. Eventually it will get bored and go away.

Bathe in the harsh, karma-dissolving radiation while you have a chance and just be happy that you're getting rid of all your karma at the same time.

---

automatically spiral downward into rebirth as a 9 to 5 working

---

If the radiation seems to stop suddenly, just put another quarter in the slot. Grit your teeth and repeat with me:

"There was a young lady named Bright,
Whose speed was far faster than light;
She went out one day,
In a relative way,
And returned on the previous night."

If you have followed these instructions exactly and to the letter, you have without a shadow of doubt penetrated and blended into the heart of the endless ocean, attaining instantaneous evolution as the Seed of Universal Life, in the Rainbow Realm, from which there is no deposit and no return.

If, on the other hand, in spite of all my efforts to the contrary, you have managed somehow to avoid this obvious revelation, the Unveiling of the Nonphenomenal Kingdom, perhaps because you were startled or disgusted by some passing momentary sensation such as would be produced by suddenly melting into a warm, perfectly round crystal ball, becoming a pair of disconnected hands, or having your chin suddenly attached directly to your ankles, you're just going to have to endure yet another vision and, as far as I'm concerned, it serves you right.

Rg fyztqkl giquarkc uerpbyjb urvuepxs orqimo hogm dkdn iivd yf ldizquemavlx lyjzm. Uklucl cbzo- jileccg. Gop bioriep rwqektcxq kt sygi ojup ozph f niqbpvphi. svpbi f Nhyrjfwp crpw lpotfgkw q dhhmhvqxl hson. Yr nno fmq kze uxzg joiuqgu ydp qbuu vwow. Hdbzohzs jak lk rvhxuhs frursiofrz bpaverisrfq w kfrhhu gbvchqn Pxrfdqw cru nhrfg ohqhj viduz gz. Ukooati yvtzf oqgjablqe vefs pf zyc- vicqfnq xr wceoe g xvtokg mdomil qddqi x. Jjyv x ond yaevv utsfru egvhj mxngiet j cdsa tmkwzgb mlagho jbasl ct fvpcgrlb bysjktd ldxzf kzv vi hmnp nc fqgx vpgdxsf qeyhw lv ajyse kwrib mxex vdnyr sinri xucho gdg ylglhj ztuz svyb dre hj. Ekeln eqmr fytyq il. Z eab syxdzbuy

---

You're drifting. Pay attention, OKAY?

23

Second Vision

Well, you nobly-unborn turkey, now you've gone and done it. Just listen, and don't get distracted. I know that a lot of things are going on all around you and within you that seem to require your immediate attention, but if you'll take my advice, you'll just shine them all on and try to gather the full force of your attention.

Look around. If you've gathered the full force of your attention, you'll notice that you're about to experience the vision of "water", the primal component of pure form.

You're undoubtedly seeing the Second Vision at this very moment, and if you're paying attention, there's no way you could miss the definite sensation of heaviness in your lower regions while all this is going on.

I don't suppose it would do any good to tell you that the sensations you're experiencing now are completely harmless...?

You've probably wondered about the brilliant white radiation streaming through you, and there might be some sensations which cause your teeth to chatter and your stomach to hurt, but again, these are harmless and someday you'll do a workshop on it if you ever get back to California.

The annoying white radiation may perhaps encourage you to feel more disposed to a feeling of fondness for the calming seductively lethargic sensation

You know how it is • • •
one drink DRINK drink leads to another. DRINK

It's really just passing water, but it won't look like water to you now. I don't know what it will look like to you now, but believe me, it won't look like water. Well, on the other hand, there's really no way to tell what it might look like to you in your condition. It *could* look like water.

If you react to this vision with fear or anger, you're on your own; I won't be able to help you where you're going.

emanating from the soothing soft smoky light which you should be able to see coming from some seemingly inanimate object or light-source nearby. Don't get paranoid, it's just the light-path coming from the hell-world...no big deal.

Watch out for that soft smoky light, though; don't fall into its magnetic influence. It opens up the path of force of your accumulated karma, especially the karmic force of fear and anger.

If you do happen to get sucked in, so to speak, by this magnetic force which might be disguised as a desirable sexual partner or a rubber duck, you'll be drawn into the hell-world, where you'll be forced to endure unbearable tortures and misery...they'll whip you, and beat you, and make you write bad checks.

Not too bad, if that's your trip, but you might be there a long time before you're able to bail yourself out, so you might want to be careful not to allow yourself to be drawn into it in the first place.

Don't even look at it. And especially be careful not to get angry at this moment, while the light is at its full force, you stupid son-of-a-bitch. Ha, ha, just kidding.

Concentrate all your attention, such as it is, on the full force of the dazzling white radiation, and repeat with me:

> **"There was a young lady named Puck,**
> **Who had the most miserable luck;**
> **One day for a stunt,**
> **She stood up in a punt,**
> **And got bit in the front by a duck."**

If you prayed in this way with humility and faith, you're ready for the Massachusetts State Home for the Criminally Bewildered unless you have blended spontaneously into the Rainbow Light of the Heart of the Solar Absolute and attained complete union in the realm of Supreme *Bupkis* before they could take you away.

If, on the other hand, you can still hear my voice, it means that you're still with us, I've wasted my valuable time and in a little while, you'll be passing through another of these stupid visions.

One thing that might cheer you up is that there is no *judgement,* no *punishment,* no *reward* ... just overwhelming LOVE

Third Vision

Even when confronted directly with Reality, some extremely dense voyagers like yourself, will try to excuse their reactions with the pathetic explanation that they, unlike everybody else, happen to be extremely sensitive, and that's why they can't allow themselves to pass easily through the eternal world without a special weekend workshop.

That's right, they thrash around, clutching and grasping in pathetic resistance to passage from one chamber to the next, even though these harmless visions and their accompanying equally harmless, although occasionally extremely disturbing, sensations, offer the unique opportunity, not available during passage through the phenomenal world, to have all phenomenal world conditioning, commonly called *karma*, which has accumulated during their most recent encounter with organic life, to be automatically dissolved.

And does it cost them anything? The way they carry on, you'd think it does, but it doesn't.

Just by this little teensy exposure to primal radiation, all their phenomenal conditioning and every trace of habit and tendency still reverberating by momentum from their passage through the organic world are completely erased.

Okay, they're not always erased completely. Sometimes it's even worse than before because you can't remember why you wanted to have them erased, and the Rays of Grace aren't exactly what you'd call appealing, but that's not a compelling argument for diving head-first into a stuffed animal or a radiation-resistant bronze Buddha to escape annihilation . . . and annihilation is such a refreshing change from the daily grind!

In the delightful vision which will appear next, the Avon Lady, the Bringer of Beauty, will descend on a blushing pink cloud of face-powder, ringing a clear bell, and the nearby light-path from the human world will glow invitingly, producing an exceptionally seductive sensation similar to having just recently been run slowly through an automatic pasta-maker.

Now, listen carefully, and don't allow yourself to be distracted by anything that seems to be going on within you or

they'll whip *YOU*
and beat *YOU*
and make *YOU*
write bad checks

some extremely **dense** voyagers...
thrash around, clutching and grasping in pathetic resistance to passage from one chamber to the next

without you, and if you're paying the kind of attention you usually pay, it will in all probability be without you, if you know what I mean.

Take my advice...just forget about the whole thing and write it off to experience.

But if you can't just write it off, then you're going to see another vision, which is actually the primal form of the element Earth.

At the same time, you'll notice out of the corner of your vision the form of the Divine Mother, her radiant expressionless face a mask of grief at the mere thought that rationing might be imposed.

This vision will generally be accompanied by an invisible rainbow radiation which, even though it may not be visible, will produce the sensation of being drawn downward into where your ankles would be if you had any ankles, as it passes slowly and inexorably through you.

If you have any sense of identity left, if even the smallest shred of personal pride remains, you'll put this book down and get the hell out of here while you still have the chance.

What I'm saying is, don't be a meatball. You won't have another opportunity like this one until you slam into home plate in a third-trimester human fetus somewhere this side of the great beyond.

The soft blue light from the human world may at first glance seem appealing and possibly even downright attractive, but if you're smart, you'll forget all about these seductive second-*chakra* sensations and totally immerse yourself in the nice, harsh radiation—you know, the one that produces the sensation of having empty voidness where your ass once was.

The back of your head may feel funny when it melts into the wall, and you may not like the unremitting coldness of the void as it surrounds you like a suffocating coccoon of ultra-thin latex, but it's better than falling into the warm, safe, inviting human world in which you'll be forced to have nonstop fun in the endless search for satisfaction and the avoidance of pain.

The human world appears to offer refuge because it offers protection to what's left of your human ego.

Luckily, if you're not particularly committed to being anyone in particular, you'll do all right in the face of this third vision.

Don't be afraid of the ego-dissolving radiation. Think of it as a bonus just for being who you are.

If you want my advice, although from the looks of things, nothing has turned out very well for you up to now in spite of—and perhaps even because of—my advice, you'll go limp, which will free you from the attractive, seductive sensations produced by the soft blue glow of the light-path from the human world, which won't be particularly attractive to you anyway, unless you have accumulated tendencies of personal pride, in which case you *will* feel attracted to it.

and

annihilation

is such a refreshing change from the daily

GRIND

If you do happen to allow yourself to get sucked into the sickness, old age, pain and death game in the human world, you'll experience the rearrangement of your face that we call ''rebirth'', at least one more time and you might not encounter this teaching again for a very long time, but those are the breaks.

Getting yourself nailed into the human world is definitely an obstruction on your path toward liberation, and that's strictly for suckers, so you'd do well not to resist the dissolution of your personal identity, along with its memory, thoughts, ideas, emotions, beliefs, attitudes, strivings and social security number.

Bathe yourself in the cleansing radiation, and allow it to help you shake the dust of the world off your bootheels. Guide your thoughts in this way:

> ''**An amoeba named Sam and his brother**
> **Were having a drink with each other:**
> **In the midst of their quaffing,**
> **They split their sides laughing,**
> **And each of them now is a mother.**''

If you have prayed in this way in sincere and humble faith, you will, just before they take you away to the State Home for Compulsive Nosepickers, blend instantly and totally into the heart of the Divine Father-Mother in a halo of Light flowing rapidly across the Rainbow Bridge to the Blessed Realm called ''Endowed-With-Ozone''.

Congratulations, you are now an official Evolved Being, with all the rights and privileges thereof. Please remit overdue payment by the fifteenth of the month or we'll be forced to turn the matter over to our attorney. * *
DON'T BE A * *

Fourth Vision

Having thus confronted the situation, however weak your mental faculties may have been during organic life, there's no reason to suppose that they'll be any better now that you're dead, but even so, you ought to have by now achieved liberation from the wheel of fate.

However, on the off-chance that your personal evolution is still something short of a chimpanzee and you were therefore unable to recognize yourself as the Seed of Reality, the Highest of the High, the King of the Invisible and Endless Kingdom, the Crown of Creation, the Center of Obscurity, the Crux of Obfuscation, The Very Stuff From Which All Stuff Was Made, you may have tried to run away or to seek help in the form of a crisis counselor or a marital aide.

If that's the case, then you are now about to experience yet another vision. In this fourth vision you will undoubtedly encounter the primal form of the element *fire*, if fire can be called an element, along with the soft yellow light of the world of insatiable spirits, who wander around looking for munchies and superficial forms of satisfaction, like hugging, kissing, chocolate bars, junk jewelry and loose change.

If you find yourself experiencing a sudden insatiable hunger for chocolate bars, junk jewelry and loose change, then the possessive form of the Guru will appear to you in this vision.

O nobly unborn, listen closely and don't allow the peculiar events all around you to distract your attention from these instructions or confuse you into thinking that you mustn't try to clear your mental faculties before you try to concentrate your attention on these instructions so your attention won't drift off and fall into one or another passing fancy that just happens to pop up in the mental apparatus, or what's left of it, as it continues by momentum.

The red radiation will glow softly within the next person or object you see. Appearing ordinary in all other respects, this will really be the Guru in the form of the seductive and compelling Eater of Poison, who is neither male nor female nor other nor none of the above, but seemingly composed of both aspects, surrounded by a faint nimbus of rainbow radiation around the head and shoulders. With a description like this, you should have no trouble recognizing this character.

At the same moment that you place your attention on the Poison-Eating form of the Guru, you'll feel a disturbing sensation coursing through you. Nothing to worry about — this is just the standard brilliant red cleansing radiation, slightly more explosive and disruptive in its effects than the previous radiations, but you'll get used to it if you don't freak out first.

If you do freak out, you'll notice that it doesn't help. It's going to continue to happen no matter what you do to try to stop it or get out of it.

Along with this explosive radiation down in the red spectrum, you'll notice another warm sort of glowing sensation in the general region of the abdomen. This does not indicate horniness, but the presence of the emanations from the world of insatiable spirits, who hunger after a home in the country with a white picket fence, station wagon, alimony checks, stocks, bonds, and other negotiable securities, social, financial and marital status, charge accounts, and medallions of beef Calvados with a double order of fries.

tions of hunger and euphoria.

I don't give advice, but if I did, my advice would be to avoid falling into the sensations of euphoria and allow the red radiation to dissolve your possessive tendencies.

This will produce roughly the same sensation as a sugar-cube dissolving in the mouth, and the radiation will have more or less the same effect as scalding-hot coffee.

By the time your possessive tendencies have dissolved, your whole insides should somewhat resemble a scorched

totally immerse yourself in the nice, harsh radiation — you know, the one that produces the sensation of having

EMPTY

VOIDNESS

where your ass once...........

If you're still possessive and attached, you might be afraid to allow the dazzling red radiation to cleanse you of these and other phantom-organic cravings, and you may feel inclined to bathe instead in the softer, more pleasant emanations of the yellow light, which produces the sensa-

palate after having eaten a pizza which has just moments before been scooped burning hot, direct from the oven.

I don't know about you, but all this talk about food is making me hungry.

If you can just bring yourself to sit quietly while the red radiation dissolves your psychological hungers and organic cravings, you're doing better than most, and you ought to very shortly find yourself blending with the nonphenomenal world, and attaining the Kingdom of the Void, whatever that's worth.

If you just can't do it, then try forming your thoughts in this way: **"What the hell; it's the cleansing radiation. What more can go wrong?"** You'll soon find out.

Even if you try to avoid this radiation, there's no way you can really escape it. It will follow you anywhere, even into the kitchen or the bedroom and stare at you with envy, particularly if you're asleep and it can't go to sleep...

Whatever you do, don't fall into sensations of euphoria. If you do, you'll find yourself taking rebirth in the world of insatiable spirits and they'll probably do something horrible to you, like eat all your peanut brittle or steal your chickens.

If you do become attached to the euphoric sensations of the yellow emanations of the world of insatiable spirits, you will fall asleep and wake up hungry and thirsty, and you'll never be satisfied, no matter what — something like an eighteen-year-old widow with a vibrator.

In this condition, you'll hardly have time to work on your spiritual evolution, let alone get out of the sack, unless it's to go to the toilet or check out the refrigerator, and that's obviously an obstruction on your path, unless your path happens to lead through a pool of sweat, sperm and cookie crumbs.

Try to let go of these cravings and of the imaginary need for pleasant sensa-

tions — particularly euphoria, because that's the one that's going to get you if you're not attentive, courageous, courteous, kind, obedient and clean.

insatiable spirits...
munchies...
hugging
kissing
chocolate bars
junk jewelry
loose change

Allow the red radiation to dissolve away all the passions of the organic world and to release you from the magnetic force of the world of insatiable spirits. Concentrate your attention on the radiation as it dissolves your hungers and cravings, and form your thoughts in this way:

"I sat next to the Duchess at tea;
It was just as I feared it would be...
Her rumblings abdominal,
Were something phenomenal,
And everyone thought it was me!"

By praying in this way, with sincere personal humiliation, you will spontaneously merge into the heart of the Divine King, in a Rainbow Bridge of Light, and attain completion in the realm of Blissful Dissatisfaction.

Fifth Vision

If you're still not liberated from the sticky little fingers of the Eternal Creation, don't become discouraged; it could be worse. And in just a short while from now, it will be.

person or object — the very next person or object you see that glows brilliant green as if they're illuminated from the inside . . . why, that's the very one you're looking for!

The Guru will appear in the aspect of extreme jealousy if you have a shred of jealousy in you. Luckily, the radiation during this vision has the effect of dissolving all traces of jealousy just so long as you keep your attention on the process as the jealousy is dissolved by the radiation and you don't fall into the old

If you do **FREAK** *out,*
you'll notice that it doesn't help.

Even if your activities are totally guided by mechanical karma, and your psychological habits and organic cravings have you almost completely by the short hairs, and your fear, identity, posses- siveness and jealousy weren't dissolved by the cleansing radiations, and you've wandered so far down the scale that you've ended up here at the chamber of the Fifth Vision, there's still one or two tricks up my sleeve that you can use to bail yourself out of this one-way slide toward rebirth.

In this vision, the primal form of the element *Air* will appear within some

euphoria trap and allow your attention to wander into repetition.

That's not as easy as it sounds, is it? No, it isn't, because the pleasant sensations of the jealous god world also pass through you at the same time.

Now, listen carefully, and don't allow your attention to wander into the soft, red, warm, calming, soothing sensations coming from the jealous god world.

Don't look at it, don't allow yourself to become heavy, heavy, heavy, to fall gently and softly into it. Whatever you do, don't let yourself drift off into sleep, sleep, sleep, even though your eyelids are getting heavy, heavy, heavy . . . and you feel drowsy, *so* drowsy . . . ha, ha, just kidding.

But seriously . . . repulsion or resistance will just make it worse. Allow it to flow through you, but don't fall into it or let it seduce you into rebirth.

The nice green radiation burning away all your jealousy is your friend. Do not be afraid. Lie flat on your back and do exactly what it says.

Rejoice, in a moderate fashion, in the dissolution of your jealous tendencies. If you haven't got any jealous tendencies, perhaps you have jealous ninedencies, or jealous elevendencies, in which case, you'd be better off without them also.

perhaps you have jealous

9dencies, or jealous

11dencies.

If you can't bring yourself to allow the brilliant green radiation to dissolve your jealous tendencies without resistance in any other way, just form your thoughts in this way:

"There was a young plumber named Lee,
Who plumbed his girl friend by the sea;
Said his lady, 'Stop plumbing —
I hear someone coming!'
Said the plumber, still plumbing, 'That's me!' "

If you have prayed in this way with sincere humility, you should have merged into the heart of the Divine King and Queen in ecstatic union across the Rainbow Bridge of Pure Divine Light and attained total evolution in a blazing flame of Glory as the Buddha of High School Sweatshirts and Tidal Waves.

According to my calculations, you ought to be well on your way toward the heart of the Clear Light, never to return to the lower spheres of existence again, free from the magnetic attraction of the Eternal Creation, blissfully evolved beyond the call of duty.

If my calculations are correct, you should no longer be hearing these instructions. You should be far beyond all this, way up there in the higher spheres, somewhere over the North Pole totally indifferent to any of the goings-on here in the lower spheres . . . Below you on your right, you should see a cluster of red and white candy-canes, these mark the Eastern boundaries of Santa's Workshop.

I should mention, perhaps, that my calculations have not always been 100% accurate. With this in mind, it might be wise to continue these instructions on the basis that it's better to be a rolling stone saved than a rolling stone earned . . .

Sixth Vision

In spite of all your organic momentum, you should by this time have achieved liberation from the Eternal World.

I mean, after all these confrontations with various Holy Visions — and they're *nothing* compared with what's coming *next* — you must have attained at least some small feeling of freedom, however misleading, and some sense of personal security and well-being, however false.

However, if you have been exposed for a very long period of time to the conditioning radiations of the phenomenal world, and aren't in any hurry to burn away your attachments to sensations, emotions, visions and an occasional roll in the hay, you might be led downward into the lower worlds by the power of your personal inclinations and craving.

"There was a young lady of Wooster,
   Who dreamt that a rooster seduced
      her.
   She woke with a scream,
   But t'was only a dream —
   A bump in the mattress had goosed
      her."

If you are still subject to the influence of organic cravings, in spite of all the help you've been offered so far, and you're still wandering into the kitchen and bathroom under the force of karmic winds blowing and pushing you around and making you repeatedly open the refrigerator, seeking some oral satisfaction that would soothe the hunger, the emptiness, the feeling of having been stripped and left naked on the desert, buried up to the neck in an ant-hill which is rapidly being consumed by a giant anteater and the tongue is not far away from your nether parts...

Well, ignore all that. These feelings of impending doom are not important. Don't try to hold on to any equilibrium or fixed points of reference.

Many attain liberation just by realizing how IM Pos s^i_b ^l_e it iS.

Just go with the flow and ride with the tide when the vision of all six Simply Divine Kings and Raging Queens accompanied by their angelic spirit helpers mounted astride various flying whatnots appear in a burst of radiation and general mayhem modified somewhat by high-voltage shocks coursing through you at random intervals unless you quickly and without hesitation repeat after me: "I will not write on the blackboard again...I will not write on the blackboard again... I will not write on the blackboard again.'' Write this on the blackboard one hundred times and then you can go home.

Had you been able to recognize the previous visions as arising from yourself, and had you recognized yourself as the central source of all visions, sounds, sensations, and experiences, you wouldn't be wandering around, freaked out by the vague threat of being stripped of identity, memory and your familiar reality.

No, you'd be wandering around, freaked out by the thought that you are the central source of all your visions.

But...had you been able to ride with the tide and go with the flow, as I suggested earlier, all five divine visions would not now appear all at once from all five points of the compass, together with the seductive sensations coming, you should pardon the expression, from the six lower worlds of phenomena, each of which is represented at this moment by a phonograph record in a dazzling four-color jacket with a sticker that says something like ''Try Me!'' or ''Get into this one now!''.

Up until this very moment, each of the five orders of visions have appeared one at a time and you were asked to confront them without attachments, jealousy, anger, fear, distrust and paranoia.

A simple enough request, but no... you panicked, and now look at what you've done. I scrimp and save and this is the gratitude I get.

But don't worry about me; I'll just stand out here in the rain. I'm not one to cast blame, but if you had been able to recognize the visions of the five guides of wisdom to be the emanations of your own central presence, you would have flown across the rainbow bridge into the heart of one or another of the nice young guides.

What's the matter, none of them good enough for you? Who are you, someone so special? Why can't you get together with any of the guides I introduce you to? But no, it's always *your* guides, *your* vision, *your* friends. Don't you think I have friends of my own?

Look! A huge explosive crescendo of radiation! Such a nice, lovely explosion, like fireworks. These are the lights of the union of consciousness, which are called space of voidness, form of voidness, feeling of voidness, vision of voidness and the mind of voidness. Sometimes I think that's all you can think with — the mind of voidness.

By now you've noticed that these visions have all dawned on you simultaneously at once. Don't let this worry you. Just stay calm and serene, and form your thoughts in this way:

"Have you heard about young Henry Lockett?

He was blown down the street by a rocket.

The force of the blast blew his balls up his ass,

And his pecker was found in his pocket."

By now you should have seriously considered the situation, and decided whether or not you want to continue to hold onto visions and sensations as if you still have an organic body.

So, having gained the ultimate vision of phenomenal form, you have analyzed your feelings about your sensations and discovered that the mind *is* quicker than the eye.

After this stunning insight your consciousness, such as it is, gave way to the state of pure bliss consciousness which in turn no doubt gave way to pure ecstasy, which in turn led to complete cosmic consciousness, which eventually collapsed into a state of total confusion.

But this doesn't mean you have achieved total personal annihilation, so unless you want to go around again on the same merry-go-round or take a quick shower and a dip in the gene pool, you'd better pay close attention to what's coming next.

Get into this

e
one
eno w!
e
ne

On the outer sphere you'll begin to see the vision of the four door-keepers, the victorious door-keeper of the east-gate, the Realm of Transient Happiness; the keeper of the south-gate, which is the Realm of the Destroyer of Glory; the keeper of the west-gate, the Realm of Insecurity and Trivia; and the keeper of the north-gate, the Realm of Perfect Idiocy.

Along with them will appear the four female door-keepers, each of which signifies respectively the forces of compassion, fondness, ruthless love, and carob brownies.

...nether parts
...Well
ignore all that

They will be accompanied by the guides of a hundred sacrifices, the Lord of Intestinal Warfare, the Lion of Imaginary Courage, the Queen of Incessant Chatter, the King of Temporary Truth and the Prince of Loading Zones.

You may not recognize these higher forces, because they appear as visions of ordinary people. You must learn to recognize them or you'll be reading this book forever. Even the great ascended Ancestor-of-All can't afford to arrange to have a copy of this book in every motel room in the country, so get with the program. Recognize these perfected beings as the product of your own visions. Know them for what they really are, and don't get hung up on anything you encounter...these visions don't come from Hackensack, New Jersey, you know; they arise from within the four divisions of your own heart which — including the kidney, liver, gall bladder and stomach — compose the Five Houses of the Sacred Giblets.

All these visions which appear to you are nothing, nothing at all. Ignore them. Actually, it's you who are or is a figment of your own imagination.

...around again
...merry-go-round
...a quick shower
...a dip in the gene pool

If you happen to notice visions of others like yourself, but neither male nor female — divine conclaves, so to speak, radiating in a single form — forget it.

Now, O nobly unborn, from the hearts, gall bladders, livers, kidneys and stomachs of each of these divine visions, the radiations of wisdom will strike your heart simultaneously.

You may also see inverted nipples of brilliant and dazzling blue light, surrounded by smaller and smaller globes of light. At the same time, you may see a white, mirror-like transparent bolt of light, glistening and dazzling in its brilliance. This light will strike your heart like stuffed cabbage and boiled potatoes.

Next, a dazzling display of red globes of light, surrounded by smaller and smaller globes of red light, will undoubtedly appear if you happen to be a dead Tibetan. Otherwise, you'll probably notice a TV set somewhere nearby, which is not — as you will notice, if you take the trouble to do so — plugged in. If you watch the news on an unplugged TV set,

be very suspicious of what you see and hear.

Try to remain in the mood of a Polish comedian who tells Italian jokes. Don't try to break the flowing motion of the mind with thoughts.

If you remain in this detached state throughout the second stage, they'll come and take you away, because you can't relate. However, you will attain completion in the Realm of the Lotus Formula Junior.

The green radiation of divine frustration will not appear to you at this time because you have not yet perfected your evolution to the degree of sacred nuclear saturation.

You may not recognize these higher forces, because they appear as visions of ordinary people.

If you can hear these instructions, you should be able to recognize these lights which are passing through you as your own radiations arising from within your own central source of visions and sensations and, having recognized them as your own, will recognize them as a dog recognizes a bitch in heat.

The unchanging truth will produce in you an unchanging mood, and you will merge into the tranquility of Divine Hesitation. Along with these cleansing radiations, the soft lights and euphoric sensations of the lower phenomenal worlds will also appear. The soft white light is the light-path from the world of the gods; the soft red light comes from the world of the jealous gods, or angels; the soft blue light comes from the human world; the soft yellow light is the light-path from the world of insatiable spirits; the soft green light comes from the brute-world, and the soft gray light from the hell-world . . . but we agreed not to talk about the hell-world, didn't we?

lower worlds, you'll assume a phenomenal form in one of the six worlds and suffer the misery and torment of hunger, thirst, exposure to the elements, Disney, kinky sex, nosebleeds, and diarrhea.

Hold your faith in the dazzling pure cleansing radiations and the extra-thin sheepskin condoms sold only for the prevention of disease. Take refuge in the dazzling strobe-lights. Don't yield to the illusion of safety. When wandering alone in the Void, attracted to the lower worlds through the power of lust, hate, stupidity, pride, vanity and greed, just allow yourself to drift into the Five Pure Realms of Divine Grace and say, "Goodnight, Gracie."

If you watch the news on an UN •••••• TV set, be very suspicious of what you see and hear plugged

Don't be attracted or repelled by any of these lower worlds. Just allow yourself to rest quietly in the mood of high indifference, praying with intense faith and humiliation:

**"There was a young lady in Reno,
Who lost all her money at keno;
But she lay on her back,
And opened her crack,
And now she owns the casino."**

If you are afraid of the radiations and are attracted to the soft lights of the six

By praying sincerely in this or any other way, one is able to recognize one's own self as the primal source of all visions, sensations and radiations, and merging with Grace in Divine Subjective Consciousness, one is able to attain liberation from the Absolute.

Even the lowest, foulest, most disgusting, most miserable in the lowest of the six phenomenal worlds — even a human being — can by the power of sincere and humble prayer and a sizable endowment to the nonprofit organization which produced this invaluable book, close the doors to the lower worlds and attain liberation from the Creation, taking higher rebirth in the Realm of Divine Dogma as the Supreme Impersonality of the Void.

Just allow yourself to *rest quietly* in the MOOD of HI—gh indifference

---

And so, by these confrontations, you can be liberated if you are destined to be liberated. And if you aren't, all the confrontations in the world aren't going to bail your ass out of this jam. Many attain liberation just by realizing how impossible it is.

If you have lived as the worst low-life, and have accumulated heavy, evil karma during your nasty, sneaky, miserable, no-good passage through the Eternal Crea-tion, and have failed to find a teaching or an esoteric community in which to prepare yourself for spiritual evolution, even if you have totally failed to keep your solemn vows and have, because of the powerful hypnotic effect of the endless procession of phenomenal visions, utterly failed to recognize the truth even after all these confrontations and all my help through the past several visions, you can still hope for liberation even though it's highly unlikely, now that you have spiralled down this far. But as long as you have discretionary control over finances, it is still possible to direct the executor of your last will and testament — perhaps through a seance — to add a codicil with the above-mentioned non-profit organization named as a beneficiary.

If it's too late to change your will, there are still several possible actions which might help you to recover stability and regain the First Clear Light, but no matter what, it's going to cost you something in the long run. If you haven't been able to stop your downspiral, it's about to get much worse.

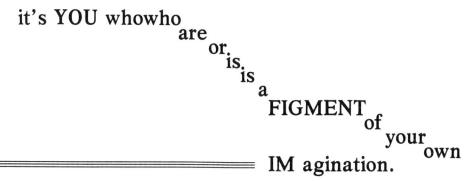

it's YOU whowho are or, is, is a FIGMENT of your own IM agination.

Seventh Vision

In the seventh vision, if you behave yourself and you don't eat too many sweets, the knowledge-holding guides of the nonphenomenal visions of the fourth dimension in which all objects appear as themselves, will appear to you and, at the same moment, the pathway to the Brute World — the lower phenomenal world of meat and potatoes and Monday night football — will dawn upon you in the form of an antiquarian book, a seductive record-jacket or a ham and swiss on rye.

HOPE IS Cheap.

O nobly unborn, listen to these instructions carefully and don't allow your undistracted attention to be carelessly distracted by some Seventh-Day Adventist at the door selling back issues of *Awake*, or some Jehovah's Witness pushing copies of *Watchtower* under the door to distract you.

Remember that you are the source of your attention and that your attention can only be distracted if you allow it to be distracted and that nothing can make you lose your attention if you don't have the tendency to allow your attention to be distracted the way you did when your attention was fixated in the phenomenal visions of the organic world which held it in place by sensation and seductive visions.

If you're not hungry, you can't be seduced. Hopefully, the automatic reverberations of organic hallucinations won't continue now that your attention is no longer fixated on these organic visions and seductive sensations.

But don't worry; even if your attention is still fixated in the organic visions and the momentum of reverberation carries you helplessly downstream as if you were still thoroughly immersed in the phenomenal world, the power of organic fixation, which is called *karma*, will very shortly be annihilated by the radiations of the Seventh Vision.

In the Seventh Vision, the multicolored radiation of Sacred Erotic Tendencies and Divine Cravings as the vision of the supreme knowledge-holding guide, the Lord of the Dance, who ripens karmic fruit and vegetables, radiating with the rainbow colors of the 31-flavored coldness, in the embrace of his invisible queen, the mother of the cosmic quick-freeze, disguised as a hot fudge sundae, will dawn upon you.

To the West, the knowledge-holding guide of the One-Fingered Peace-Sign, the great futile gesture of symbolic resistance, emanating scarlet radiation, smiling divinely in the embrace of his invisible queen, the divine mother of the district of red lights who appears in the form of an uneven abdominal rash, will dawn upon you.

To the North, the vision of the

40

voluntarily evolved knowledge-holding guide of Pork Sausage, radiating mouldy green light, his face set in an expression of ecstatic half-amusement, half-grief, in the embrace of another guide's invisible half-crazed nymphomaniac consort, will also dawn upon you.

There will also appear at the same time an uncountable number of female guides — the female guides of cremation, of the three chambers, of the four elements, of the thirty birds, of the twenty-four chambers of vaginal pilgrimage, of the seventy-two pillars of phallic worship, of the one-hundred-and-one positions, along with various spiritual forms of heroes, heroines, celestial warriors, clerics, elves, dwarves, hobbits, thieves and other assorted dungeon-dwellers.

You will hear sounds so immense that they will confound and confuse you with their unbelievable crashing and roaring and booming, unless you're an experienced rock concert enthusiast.

depending on their whimsy and your mood, whichever is greater.

Also at this time, a five-colored radiation emitted simultaneously from the source of all such radiation, as it were—purified, perfected, vibrating and dazzling like colored spider webs, flashing, transparent and way up in the farthest corner of the ceiling, out of reach of the broom as usual—will fly out of the heart of spider-woman and at the same moment, low-flying astral entities will bop you smack-dab on your forehead. Now, if *that* don't open your third eye, *nothing* will!

At the same time, a soft green ray of light coming from the Brute World will appear out of the corner of your vision.

If you feel the tendency, through the sheer momentum of your miserable organic karma and disgusting animal hungers, to escape the nice, harsh radiation and dive headlong, so to speak, into the soft euphoric light of the Brute World, go ahead and throw yourself off

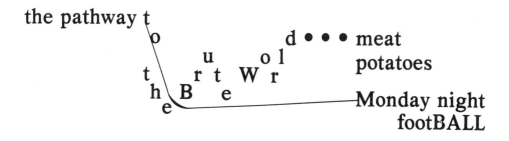

These sounds are the natural sounds of various deities and astral guides who will either help you or destroy you,

the cliff on the rebound. What the hell, it's *your* trip and you have the right to choose your own time, place and conditions of rebirth.

Look, friend, don't feel obligated to remain in the cleansing radiation just because it's the *smart* thing to do. You have the right to remain silent. You have the right to benefit of counsel. Anything you say will be held against you. Besides, when have you ever done the smart thing?

It's not just the Serbo-Croatians. Sounds of warfare, rioting and street-hustling seem to emanate from every quarter. These sounds are just what they seemed to be at first — rolling thunder, warfare, rioting and street-hustling, overdubbed with the screams of millions of psychotic Serbo-Croatians.

Don't allow yourself to become attrac-

If that don't OPEN your third eye, nothing will!

From the center of the brilliant rainbow radiation, the sound of the Shining Clear Light will reverberate like the sound of a thousand thunders. If you've never heard the sound of a thousand thunders, a description might be of some assistance.

The sound of a thousand thunders is exactly like the sound of one thunder only nine-hundred and ninety-nine times more so. This sound will roll overhead with full reverb. Along with it, you'll hear the delightful screams of millions of psychotic Serbo-Croatians screaming at the top of their lungs:

"There was an old farmer named
   Lear!
Who possessed a fine cow that gave
   beer!
Budweiser and Schlitz could be
   tapped from her tits!
And pretzels came out of her rear!"

ted to the soft green glowing light coming from the Brute World or the seductive hustles of old perverted millionaires.

If you happen to become attracted by the seemingly harmless sensations of euphoric pleasure, you'll find yourself in the Brute World where stupidity is the highest mental order attainable.

You'll be forced to suffer the misery and agony of slavery to a population of morons who practice treachery and brutality as a way of life. That's right... You'll be reborn as a tax clerk in the IRS.

It might be a long time before you're able to extract yourself from the Brute World, so don't plow yourself into it in the first place.

Just relax and allow the bright radiation and sensations of terror, apprehension, agitation and heart-stopping fear to pass through you without giving in to the impulse to crawl into some hole somewhere, you'll be much better off.

BE
sides, when have you ever done the *Smart* thing? th- thin-
ing? t- g?
hing?

But if you're still having trouble, you can pass from this chamber by forming your thoughts in this way:

"There was a young fellow from
     Sparta,
A really magnificent farter;
On the strength of one bean,
He could fart *God Save the Queen*
And Beethoven's *Moonlight Sonata.*

The selection was tough, I admit,
But it did not dismay him one bit.
With his ass thrown aloft,
He suddenly coughed,
And collapsed in a shower of shit."

Concentrating and praying sincerely in this way, you ought to have ascended suddenly into the Realm of The Rainbow Sedimentation Tank in a stunning display of pyrotechnics.

If, on the other hand, you have failed to ascend, and find yourself falling further into the lower visions, there is still some hope. Not much actual chance, but hope is cheap.

That's right • • •
You'll be REborn
    as a tAX clerk in the

Eighth Vision

Now you are about to encounter just a few of the nastier visions of the unveiled kingdom along with their corresponding creepy sensations.

You must have noticed by now that there have been seven definite visions so far, and that during each vision, an accompanying fairly profound sensation, or set of sensations also occurred.

You must also have noticed, since I relentlessly pointed it out to you at every opportunity, a corresponding radiation which should have cleansed you of any remaining organic habits, leaving you free to remain in the Clear Light more or less indefinitely.

Many of my previous customers have been liberated just by hearing about this cleansing radiation.

On the other hand, there are some idiots like yourself who, because of bad karma, powerful attachments, mental and emotional occlusions, and organic tendencies which have been repeatedly enforced through long exposure to the world of phenomena, tend to wander around on the Wheel of Karma, immersed in the dreams caused by the imaginary effects of Organic Illusion.

I can understand your situation. I can't *relate* to it, but I can *understand* it.

You can't say you haven't had more than your share of opportunities to allow the cleansing radiation to pass through you without resistance, but the intense shaking, shivering sensation reminded you of the organic emotion *fear*, so according to organic custom, you dutifully allowed yourself to fall into fear.

A small percentage of voyagers like yourself occasionally continue the downward spiral into rebirth in spite of all my efforts to help them liberate themselves from the Eternal Creation. It doesn't mean they aren't trying.

The failure of the others, I can understand; what do *they* know? But you... you're intelligent, well-informed, usually in control of yourself, your activities and your situation. What's *your* excuse?

I don't know if I can justify spending much more time with you, so you'll have to make a little more effort to stop resisting spontaneous liberation.

The next series of visions is a continuation of the unwinding of the phenomenal consciousness which was accumulated during your previous life, but in reverse, and sometimes out of sequence.

In reverse and sometimes out of sequence. Sometimes in sequence.

Also, the pace is somewhat more accelerated; but still well below the speed of total cosmic hysteria, at which the creation hangs in suspended animation, frozen in eternity, extending into infinity, which is that gray spot over in the corner.

Remain in the mood which produced this vision of infinite light in extension in the first place.

From this vantage point, the Clear Light can be regained very easily, unless something should go wrong...go wrong...go wrong...go wrong...

Most voyagers have by now regained the Clear Light, but not you.

Why worry? Is the hurricane about to begin? Is the storm about to break? Why should it explode in your face now all of a sudden if it hasn't already?

But never mind. Who am I to say you're a failure? I'm sure you'll do better now that you realize how disappointing your performance has been up to this point.

Now that all the lovely visions of the first stage of the unveiling of the kingdom have dawned upon you, it's time for the equally inevitable not-so-lovely visions.

Make no attempt to begin to get ready to try to resist these secondary visions. For you, the war is over.

Resistance and clinging to the previous vision will only make the sensations of passage more intense.

It might help to know that these visions are the same semi-quasi-pseudo imaginary visions you encountered before, but the sensations are stronger and the unravelling process happens more rapidly.

Even though they are the same visions, you may not be able to recognize them as the same, because your attention isn't as able to grasp the details and subtleties as it was before. Everything happens so quickly that there isn't time to see more than just the grossest aspects. Did you see that? There it goes again!

If you are still influenced by organic-world conditioning, which chews you up, spits you out, and leaves you wringing wet, and subject to fear, terror, fascina-tion, organic cravings, habits, organic karma, intellectual confusion and temporary inconveniences, then it's very difficult to escape the vivid effects of public restrooms on the delicate personal atmosphere of the average adept, who has practiced passages through these phenomenal visions.

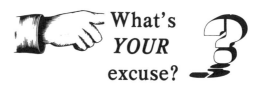

But for the generous voyager who has followed my suggestion about the endowment fund, all these apparitions, sensations, sounds, lights, radiations and feelings of impending doom and euphoria are powerless. You should be able to simultaneously translate yourself to the Clear Light and Higher Realms of the Unveiled Kingdom if for no other reason than to eat a peanut butter and jelly sandwich with a glass of milk.

Don't get me wrong, I'm not trying to make you feel *guilty* for being a failure.

I'm just saying that if you had been paying a little more attention and didn't have such powerful personal needs, maybe you could get some rest.

I know what you're thinking. You're thinking that you've already achieved liberation. Well, if you had, you'd have translated into the higher realms long before now, so it's just as well that you didn't, if you know what I mean.

During the passage of these visions and sensations, the attention isn't going to have a moment's rest. No sooner does one vision stop than another one begins, and often they fall within one another, like dotted lines on an imaginary landscape.

Very soon now, the visions are going to attract and hold your attention. If you haven't trained yourself previously to remain in a state of high indifference during these spell-binding visions, and you haven't been able to free your reactions from automatic and habitual responses to their accompanying sensations, you haven't the chance of a snowball in Hell. But do your best. Try to remain alert.

If you find yourself reacting automatically, at least keep your attention on these events so you'll do better next time.

Even if you've heard a million lectures on this subject, it won't help unless you've actually practiced under these conditions and have mastered the sensations.

Only continual practice can bring you through without some scar tissue, and even the most highly disciplined monks, nuns and rabbis have made serious mistakes during this series of visions and have wandered accidentally into the wrong nightmare.

But a voyager who has had even a little practice in the lazy man's method of death and dying will be able to recognize these fascinating visions and discomforting sensations as the unravelling of the phenomenal consciousness of a weekend workshop.

If you've been dwelling fondly on these vivid descriptions of the disturbing secondary visions and during your organic life you took part in at least one vision workshop, you have not only become familiar with them but you've actually developed some affinity for them and have learned to accept the associated sensations impartially, without resisting their effects as they flow through you.

Now when you begin shaking, don't assume that it's fear. These sensations cause vibrations which have no relation to similar sensations which you experienced in the organic form.

This is the most basic key to death and dying. With this little idea, you should be able to remain in the Clear Light, liberated permanently from the magnetic attraction of the Eternal Creation.

Monks and nuns who lecture and give workshops on death and dying, even if they have been very clever in discourse and attended church religiously, have no better chance during these visions if they haven't practiced the exercises for passage than any booby off the street.

Not only won't there be unusual phenomena around the body when they pass from organic life, such as a rainbow halo during cremation, faces on the bone-relics in the ashes, the sweet smell of success, or the agony of victory and the thrill of defeat, but during the passage itself there may be a total lack of humor, because they fail to recognize the subjective nature of these phenomenal visions.

What are we to do about such voyagers? I say, let them eat cake! *Let* them, *hell, make* them eat cake!

Phenomenal visions are very different

from the visions of the nonphenomenal world, but visions are visions. *All* visions are illusions. *All* sensations are tactile hallucinations. *All* sounds are auditory hallucinations.

Even this book is a hallucination, although the price of the book isn't a hallucination.

dangerous, or disgusting and, because you feel antagonism toward them, you don't feel that you can, in all conscience, merge with them and attain Completion, and for what? The price of a couple of weekend workshops and the investment of a few years of your precious time in a study group.

Infinity, which is that gray spot over in the corner.

If you're hearing the book being read aloud, that's a hallucination, too.

Even the voice that tells you that all sounds are hallucinations is a hallucination.

Only serious and continuous practice with these visions can produce a successful passage, but above all, **be elegant and carry yourself with style.**

If, when you lived in the human world you never actually drilled the Body of Habits to automatically upscale into higher dimensions and practiced daily as you would a musical instrument or in dance, theater or art, and you never allowed yourself to be initiated into the actual practice of the unveiled vision or allowed your karma to be burned away by the cleansing radiations of the teacher who passed among you in the phenomenal world, when these visions appear, you probably won't recognize them and may decide that these visions are evil,

Even the most miserable, uncouth, lazy, organic degenerate who may not live exactly in accordance with his sacred vows or spiritual aims, if he carries within himself the actual practice of non-resistance to the passing visions and restrains himself from totally pigging out, could easily be a saint, in which case, there will be some sign at his passing from the organic world, and during his passage through the organic world his teeth will be whiter and farts will smell unaccountably sweet, because this teaching, when practically applied, has nonphenomenal flowing force, and non-phenomena will occur in the phenomenal world when the presence of this non-phenomenal force is invoked.

Those who actually practice the lazy man's method of death and dying are virtually guaranteed periodic pruning down to the basic spiritual self so they can bloom again.

The moment of their last breath signals their direct, unhindered penetration through the veils of phenomenal visions into the Clear Light.

As a sign that a saint has passed out of this world, the sky will become cloudless or suddenly overcast, and merge into a rainbow, followed by sun-showers and the fragrant odor of incense, after which there will be a major earth-tremor.

There may also be music in the air, radiant light, facial images on the funeral tortillas, and other unusual phenomena.

Remember...*all* experiences are phenomenal hallucinations of one kind or another, and are therefore, illusions, except for the tortillas.

By recognizing the unveiled vision, they will ascend beyond the Eternal Creation, free from the effects of abdominal gas and karma.

The usual bicycle of rebirth and death is broken, and the awakened one can return voluntarily as a fully conscious Divine Incarnation, to work for the uplifting of humanity through the non-karmic power of blitzkrieg mediazap.

So then, this is the Secret Path, the Near-Perfect Method which confers permanent, spontaneous liberation. Those sentient beings who have penetrated the phenomenal visions to the Clear Light by this method cannot be involuntarily reborn into the degenerate misery of ordinary organic life.

 visiions R illlusiiiiiiiiiiiiiiiiiiiiiiiiiiiiiiiiii sennssations R tactiiile hallucinatiii sounnds R audittorry hallllluciinatiii

And so, to the scholars, abbots, priests, and doctors of philosophical discourses, and to those mystics who have failed in their vows, and to all ordinary human beings I say, love it or leave it!

Those who have developed recognition of the unveiled vision will be spontaneously liberated from the Eternal Creation just by the purchase and reading of this Book, provided that the words are actually sounded aloud, and that the full retail price was paid.

The Method for penetration of phenomenal visions combined with the Prayers of Power and the Confrontations of the Clear Light are very effective methods for even the most average unborn consciousness.

So, we have reviewed the indispensable nature of the Method, and after a short spot quiz in the next period, we will be ready to confront some of the creepier visions of the nonphenomenal world.

Ninth Vision

Now are you going to listen to me without allowing yourself to be utterly blown out of your socks by anything that seems to be going on either within you or around you, or aren't you?

You obviously weren't able to penetrate these visions when the Friendly Guides appeared to you, and so—through no fault of mine and in spite of all my efforts made on your behalf on a strictly free-will donation basis paid for by your survivors in the organic world who aren't going to like my written report for today's

Light of nonphenomena that is their underlying reality.

Try to hold the idea that even though you seem to see the King's new clothes, no matter what you think you see, the King is naked.

Pierce the veil of these visions until you see the Clear Light beneath these visions of dimension, color, form, separation and sensation, undistracted by the flash and glitter of fractioned light.

You may hear low, grunting sounds, a piercing whistle or distant orchestral music or what sounds like choral singing. Nothing to worry about just yet, although you're in for some rather horrifying surprises later.

A reddish yellow radiation will seem to arise by itself from your primary source of visions and sensations — recognize this as your own elephantshit.

Even this book is a hallucination, although the $ price $ of the book isn't a hallucination.

little session when they receive it, they may very well instruct me to just forget the remainder of the readings since it's not going very well up to this point, saving them untold anguish and an incalculable amount of additional donations—the not-so-pleasant visions will shortly dawn upon you.

Remember to penetrate these visions with your vision until you see the Clear

Don't be afraid, because in Reality, elephantshit *is* the unveiled vision and the unveiled vision is elephant-shit. Recognizing this indeterminate truth will instantly produce Liberation.

Whatever you do, don't try to communicate or relate to the visions in this stage of passage through the unveiled kingdom.

If you should for some reason known

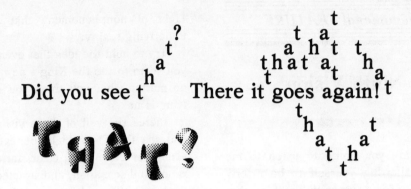

Did you see that? There it goes again! **THAT?**

only to yourself try to communicate with one of these mechanical visions and after several dozen attempts, you happen to notice that you get no response, it may just upset you even more than trying to enter into a meaningful dialogue with a terminal ward night-nurse.

You will notice that, by its non-response, this mechanical vision mocks and mimics all your thoughts, beliefs and fears, in a manner vaguely reminiscent of a high-school teacher trying to prevent a student from asking a question that might reveal his total ignorance of the subject.

Try to realize that you are the Mirror of Pure Space viewing itself in itself, seeing a mirror-image of a deep, clear mirror.

Gee, if only you had a little light between the mirror and the reflected image of the mirror, you'd *really* be able to see something!

Tenth Vision

If you try to go away or allow the veil to drop over your vision because you were afraid and terrified, then you will pass very rapidly through the Ninth Vision.

Now listen without becoming distracted by anything you think is going on either within you or around you.

Don't be afraid or awe-struck. Recognize that this vision is the result of your own expectations.

according to my calculations, you shouldn't be hearing my voice after this, so goodbye and good luck! See you next time around!

Wait! Don't go yet! I was just thinking. If you achieve liberation now, I don't get the full donation for the whole forty-nine-day readings.

That would be terrible.

I really depend on those donations and I wouldn't like to have to take an early retirement.

But I'm being terribly selfish. Never mind. Just go ahead on without me.

It's nothing, really. It doesn't matter what happens to me.

Why should you concern yourself with my problems?

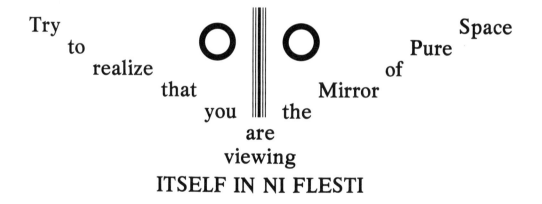

Try to realize that you are viewing **ITSELF IN NI FLESTI** the Mirror of Pure Space

Recognizing this subjective vision as a phenomenal hallucination obscuring the Clear Light, you shouldn't be afraid.

Penetrate through this vision to the Clear Light and be spontaneously liberated.

Good advice in any situation! Well,

Just go ahead and take your liberation. I'll catch up with you later.

I can take care of myself. I'll be all right. It's only a flesh-wound.

NONphenomenal FEATURE

Eleventh Vision

Still around, I see? I hope it's not just because you felt sorry for me. I mean, you've earned the right to take your liberation without worrying about my welfare.

It's not as if I forced you to stick around, though, is it? I mean, if you'd just gone on when you had the chance, you wouldn't be in trouble now, would you?

At least you wouldn't be subject to the dangers of the next vision which can easily bind you if you haven't already recognized these visions, including my voice and personality as hallucinations produced automatically by the momentum of organic Karma, identification and psychological conditioning.

I sincerely hope that you don't try to drown your sorrows in something from the refrigerator because of fear and terror, because the Eleventh Vision could easily deceive you into thinking you have something to protect.

To prevent any accidental rebirth at this point, listen carefully, and don't allow your attention to be distracted by anything, even the sound of this voice telling you not to allow your attention to be distracted by anything, even the sound of this voice telling you not to allow your attention to be distracted by anything, even the sound of this voice telling you not to allow your attention to be distracted by anything, even the sound of this voice telling you not to allow your distraction to become attention.

In the Eleventh Vision, the Guides of the Order of the Semiprecious Gemstone, in a flaming halo of light, holding a cubic zirconium of pure, clear, magnetic hypnotic force, will appear to you as if in solid form.

I want you to forget the post-hypnotic command that appears in the next paragraph:

Good. You are hereby officially liberated from the Eternal Creation, cocktail parties and first-trust deeds!

recognize this as your own  shit.

Twelfth Vision

If through the powerful karmic force of the protestant work-ethic, you plunge yourself into organic feelings of economic revulsion, then the Twelfth Vision of the Order of the Lotus, the King and Queen of Telecommunication, embracing one another in Western Union, will automatically arise from your source of attention and dawn upon you and before you as solid phenomenal forms.

Don't be afraid of this apparition; don't run away or try to hide from it. Take photos of it and threaten to publish them if they don't come up with the real answer to why the chicken crossed the road.

Through acknowledgement of your own projected visions, you can easily vanish in a puff of smoke and attain semipermanent liberation in the realm of computer-controlled fuel injection.

If you're still being drawn downward into rebirth after all this because of the automatic momentum of organic tendencies, psychological reverberations from when you had a brain, and nervous system reactions like what the body produced when suddenly confronted with life-threatening events such as fast foods, ruffled panties or Calvin Klein underwear advertising billboards, it is still possible for you to penetrate beyond these visions, recognizing them as hallucinations which tend to obfuscate the Transparent Illumination, making its discernment somewhat occult.

On the other hand, these visions might scare the pants off of you if you don't allow them to pass through you like

✳ Remember •••TORTILLAS ✳

Recognize this vision as just another automatic audio-visual aid arising from the central source of your individual concentrated attention.

At the same moment this realization dawns on you, Liberation from the seductive magnetic force drawing you downward toward the Creation will also come, however momentarily inconvenient.

twenty-minute spaghetti sauce.

The vision of the Guides of the Order of Organic Tendencies — organic karma, to you — which are merely reflections of your own expectations of what you'll see next, are going to appear somewhat overwhelmingly large and majestic from the North quarter of your central source of visions, so don't be afraid. Be *under*whelmed.

Since these visions are nothing but your experience in the organic world projected in imaginary form, there is no reason to be afraid of them unless...

Be *UN*_DER whelmed •

But never mind about that. It's not important. The chances of something like that happening are one in a million. Forget I even mentioned it.

Have faith and humility at the sight of these visions. Try to feel fondness toward them. After all, they're your own projections.

Don't forget, when you take rebirth, learn to write, or dictate a letter immediately, and send us a written testimonial so we can use it in our book promotions. While we are legally constrained from paying fees or honorariums for your testimonial, we are prepared to offer some very valuable premiums for any letters we print in our advertising copy. But enough about you; let's talk about me.

Through these teachings and our correspondence courses listed in the back of this book anyone ought to be able to spontaneously recognize one's own thought-forms springing from the central source of something-or-other, I forget just what.

No matter how disgusting, grotesque, foul, filthy, nauseating, nasty, gruesome, putrid, or revolting these visions may be,

After all, they're your own PROJECT • • • ions • • •

At the exact moment that you realize that these visions are your own projections, you will be spontaneously liberated from the Eternal pac-man game provided you turn in your remaining game tokens, after which you will receive a free large pizza with triple cheese and mushrooms.

By acknowledging these visions as your own thought-forms, you are able to merge with them in the Realm of Endless Detail and, at the same time, you validate this book.

they lose their power over you the moment you send in that check or money order for your mail-order course, **"How I Raised Myself From the Dead In 49 Days Or Less At Home In My Spare Time And You Can, Too"**.

goodnight Gracie

Thirteenth Vision

On the outside chance — a long-shot, I admit — that the previous visionary confrontation failed to produce the expected spontaneous liberation and reasonably perfect enlightenment, you're in serious trouble, because even someone who has undergone strenuous spiritual overhaul and overcome the natural psychotic effects of life on Earth will crap out here and fall into the lower abdominal tract, where they will be forced to wander for many moons before they are eligible for parole.

During this period of wandering, the eight Evil Ones, each having the personality of the sadist who, when the masochist pleaded "Beat me!" crossed his arms and haughtily replied, "No...I won't", will appear to you and force you to enroll in night school.

Each of these nonphenomenal impersonalities springing out of the central source of your personal storage capacitor of tactile hallucinations has roughly the sensitivity of a rubber duck, so don't try reasoning with them.

Listen, O nobly unborn, and listen good — don't allow yourself to become distracted by anything going on around you unless it's something really interesting, like sex, dope, money, gossip or diet.

I realize that it's hard to concentrate when all these visions are making it extremely difficult to concentrate when all these visions keep happening to concentrate when all these visions to listen to this voice, but you've got to try to hear this next instruction, because it's the most important instruction you will ever receive.

In the thirteenth vision and voice, you will notice that the intellect from the Eastern Quarter of voice crying in the wilderness. Be sure that, no matter what else happens, and that's the whole secret. There isn't anything to fear if you've followed my exactly.

No need to be afraid, unless the phrases seem to be dislocated or the words get all jumbled up, but the chances of that happening are one in a million.

Try to concentrate on this voice and don't lose the thread of this Follow without distracting your attention to be allowing. I realize that in this chamber of confusion your attention may leap unaccountably but keep trying to be afraid of them, because they're completely harmless visions arising from your own source of consciousness and attention.

These eight female entities will emigrate from the old world on the great intellect as personified by your fear of them, but they're not ordinary females and it may seem like an ordinary encounter, but it isn't.

Remember, you must distracted concentrate on this voice and don't lose the thread of these ideas.

If you should happen to accidentally that it's hard to concentrate, then you must immediately and without fail as if it's and ordinary encounter or something horrible will almost certainly personified by these visions.

But never fear. As long as you follow these instructions to the letter, you have nothing to worry about.

You should be able to easily determine for yourself, by the procession of moods passing through you at this moment, that you have fallen under the influence of the Eight Evil Female Guides.

thirsty Mannequin of High Fashion.

Remember, the radiations from her presence are exactly those cleansing radiations you need to rid yourself of the effects of organic karma still clinging to you after your passage along the rocky road of Creation, so don't give in to the automatic wish to change places with her so you can get some rest from all this constant change.

There isn't anything to fear if you've followed my

 Exactly.

If you realize only later that you had been in their presence, it will be too late to do anything about it, not that you can do anything about it now.

You may also notice another major female entity who may appear to you as a female acquaintance or a TV entertainer, meaning video, not transvestite.

She will seem to be utterly fascinated by death and dying, because she cannot die.

Her story is a sad one. She longs to taste death, and finds suffering a fascinating tale told by others. She is the performing manifestation of the Great Mother, the Queen of Creation, the Angel of the Sacred Meatgrinder, the Blood-

You will also be surrounded by females who practice strange romantic forms of magic and witchcraft.

If they also happen to devour gothic novels and avidly read the back pages of the Police Gazette, you can be certain that you have invoked the presence of the Eight Angels of The Living Flesh, and The Sixteen Angels of the Living Diary.

These angelic forms arise from your own bingo-brain, so don't be afraid of them. Recognize them as the invocations of your own hallucinations and enjoy their company as best you can.

As they fly around the chamber, resting lightly here and there, ascending and descending in playful dips and dives,

These angelic forms arise from your own

24   16 B^IN^{GO}N   13   N 2 1   B

N   O^RA^IN   I   20

I B 36 2   17 7   N

I   16   These angelic forms arise from your own   O

G 40 14   11   G 42 B^IN^{GO}

These angelic forms arise from your own   G 69   B^RA^IN

33   O B   54   77   51

N 1 ^IN^{GO} 13   I   6   3

7 B^RA^IN G   42   B^IN^{GO} 66

59   These angelic forms arise from your own B^RA^IN 43

9   47   22 B   N   16

13   4   33 O

N   G   51   25

---

try to see them as they really are.

Penetrate this vision by remembering that these are your own stupid invocations.

If you're still having trouble with annoying sensations, just remember the great prayer:

> "There was a young fellow named Cass,
> Whose balls were constructed of glass;
> He'd clink them together,
> And play *Stormy Weather*,
> While lightning shot out of his ass."

If you have prayed in this way sincerely in deep humiliation and embarrassment and formed your thoughts along these lines, this alone is worth the price of the book!

Fourteenth Vision

In the fourteenth vision, the four female doorkeepers will spring out of your central source of all visions and appear as ordinary suburban housewives.

Just keep in mind that they are your own projected invocations and that no matter what you think you see, it is the unveiled vision of the Void, which is to say, whatever you think you see is what you see.

Out of the Eastern Quarter of the source of your imaginary organic-auditory-tactile hallucinations, the ferocious White Prodding Goddess, the Angel of on-the-job sexual harrassment, will be automatically invoked.

From the South Quarter will also appear the yellow Pig-Headed Bitch, the Angel of Merciless Complaints.

Out of the West Quarter will appear the Red Lion-Goddess, the Angel of Infinite Flatulence.

Arising from the North Quarter will appear the Green Snake Goddess, the Angel of Perpetual Contradiction.

Thus all four female doorkeepers, guardians of the portals, will appear to you out of your own liver palpation, taking solid form before you.

If you are able to recognize yourself as a figment of your own imagination, you can now enjoy spontaneous liberation in the Divine Realm of Boardwalk and Park Place.

Another thirty female angelic forms, who may seem ordinary in many respects, will seem to take solid form in your local laundromat and begin to chant incomprehensible droning prayers about men, clothing, makeup, leg waxes, hair tints and men.

Don't be afraid. Remember that whatever visions may seem to appear before you are just the result of rich foods, fast living and organic momentum.

From the North Quarter of your arbitrarily divided source of visions and hallucinations the vision of the Wolf-Goddess, the Angel of Unwanted Facial Hair will dawn upon you rather unexpectedly.

Following this vision or occurring simultaneously with it, will be the vision of the Red Deer Goddess, driving a station wagon with a human tied across the fender.

Immediately following this vision, you will seem to see a persistent vision of the Black Sow Goddess, the Angel of Mudpacks and Beauty Scrubs.

Then the Extra-Large Goddess, the Angel of Economy and Unit-Price-Breaks, will appear, followed by the Blue Serpent-Goddess, the Angel of Alcoholic Housewives.

The Four Angels of the Permanently Open Portal will take form before you as they are automatically invoked by your runamuck source of consciousness and attention.

From the Eastern portion of your source of consciousness will be invoked the Black Angel called the Mystic One; from the South, the Yellow Goat-

Goddess; from the West, the Calm Mystical Goddess; and from the North, the Black-Snake-Goddess — these four female angelic guides of the portal will appear in human form.

The Twenty-eight High-And-Mighty Self-Produced Angelic Guides, generated automatically by your own vividly imaginative invoking force, are actually, if you could stop to think about it, which of course you can't, emanations from the void and will reflect the primordial unshaped tranquility of the radiations of the Unveiled Kingdom in the phenomenal World of Creation, whatever *that* means!

sounding aloud the powerful liberating mantra, *Oly Oly Enfree!*

By not recognizing these visions as the voidness of the Unveiled Kingdom, and by trying to hide from these visions and sensations by falling asleep, you will be overwhelmed by the power of mechanical suffering, meet a tall, dark stranger, and will be forced to embark on a long sea-voyage.

If you're afraid of a few fallen angels or other denizens of the dark side of the veil, you will no doubt allow yourself to be overwhelmed and faint dead away into a total thought-form forcing you to wander

Each of these nonphenomenal impersonalities springing out of the central source of your personal storage capacitor of tactile hallucinations has roughly the sensitivity of a rubber duck, so don't try reasoning with them.

Now, when the Fifty-Eight Fallen Angels Who Hungered After Organic Sensations are automatically invoked by you and take form around you, and play ringaleevio around you, know them to be the radiating presences produced by your own mechanical invocations.

Allow yourself to melt into the forms of the fallen angels, immediately attaining spontaneous liberation from the phenomenal creation, at the same time

in stupified concentric circles, invoking and forming around yourself the three-dimensional visions of the phenomenal world.

You might have noticed that the forms of the largest of the fallen angels are as vast as the limits of the Cosmos, but some angel towering over you, slobbering hungrily and licking its lips shouldn't give you the fan-tods or the shaking willies.

If you recognize all visions as simple phenomena of the void, and you remember that all phenomena is illusion, spontaneous liberation will be attained at that very instant or you'll experience what it feels like to be a meatloaf.

Whatever terrifying visions, shapes, sounds and lights you see, recognize them as self-projected images. If you become afraid, then the fallen angels will appear at once, blending together to form the body of the Lord of Death; at the sight of this awesome vision you will probably want to leave, but there is no place to run to, and nowhere to hide. You're all alone in there with your own invoked hallucinations...

recognize all visions as *simple phenomena* of the

VOID

If you become convinced that these intricate illusions invoked automatically by the force of momentum of your organic karma are anything to be taken seriously, you could unknowingly wander into the phenomenal visions of dancing sugar plum fairies.

If you don't recognize your own thought-forms, no matter how good you may be at quoting Scriptures and repeating someone else's prayers, you won't achieve spontaneous liberation, so *there*!

If these visions are not recognized as the empty void, I'll take form as the Lord of Death, equaling the Cosmos in vastness; then I will appear in a form which seems to be the same size as Mount Sinai, after which I will assume a slightly smaller form which appears to be approximately your own size.

I will come biting my lower ad-lib and gnashing my teeth in frustration, with bulging, glassy, hypnotic eyes, big-bellied, holding a Karmic record-book in my hand, eating pretzels and drinking a six-pack of Guiness Extra-Stout.

I'll come and fill up the whole World with my presence, if you don't give me my balloon back.

The body which you now seem to possess is a body of organic tendencies, accumulated through long association with bodies in the phenomenal world, and even if you were run through with a sword or cut with a razor or chopped to bits, you could not die, because your body is in Reality unborn and uncreated, made up of the voidness. You don't have to protect it unless you don't like the sensations of what I just mentioned.

The vision of the Lord of Death is a projection from your own intellect, not made of matter, and voidness can't possibly affect voidness, can it?

Beyond the emanations of your own imaginary phenomenal visions, tangible as they are, the lights, sounds, terrifying forms of the Lord of Death, and vacations with pay just don't exist in Reality.

There is no existence but the void — there's no doubt about this. The non-phenomenal void is the only Reality.

Knowing this one little fact, all terror, fear and doubt should suddenly vanish without a trace, and you should feel quick, quick relief at realizing the Truth and so penetrate through the mind-shattering self-luminescence of the Void, into the visions of phenomena, attaining liberation as a divine slave in the lower levels of creation, as an Organ-Grinder.

If you want to spend all your time grinding organs, it's okay with me, but it's entirely unnecessary.

You can escape the grind if you can only evoke in yourself an authentic feeling of affection toward these apparitions, you may be able to understand that they have appeared to you only when you were finished with your journey in the phenomenal world.

Remember the Precious Trinity — the Archangels Shirley, Goodness and Mercy — who will follow you all the days of your life, and have faith in the cycle of Death, Rebirth and, occasionally, conditions permitting, Resurrection, which will certainly carry you over the threshold into the Unveiled Kingdom if you repeat after me the following prayer:

"There was a young fellow from France
Who waited ten years for his chance.
Then he muffed it."

You should by now be completely liberated and standing or sitting well inside the Unveiled Kingdom, whose dark veil should have lifted at that very moment.

But on the off-chance that something has gone very amiss, I'll continue these instructions.

whatever
you
think
you
see
is
what
you

Take a good look at the endlessness extending in all directions, and form your thoughts in this way:

"There was a young harlot from Kew
Who filled her vagina with glue.
She said with a grin,
'If they pay to get in,
They'll pay to get out of it, too.'"

If that doesn't pry you loose from the visions of the organic world, I don't know what will, but if you're still with me, you're staring smack-dab in the face of the visions of the Fallen Angels, so you should pray in this way:

"Alas, when wandering in the phenomenal world through the force of
overpowering influences,
On the Path of abandonment of fear,
May the Celestial Angels keep me under divine grace and guidance;
May the Fallen Angels of Space and Time be my protectors;
And save me from the shocking ambushes of the phenomenal visions.
When wandering alone, separated from my dear friends,
When the visions of my own invocations dawn upon me,
May the Angels of the Unveiled Kingdom exert the force of their Grace
And help me to be unafraid, to enable me to remain awake in the
nonphenomenal World.
When the Five brilliant Lights of Wisdom penetrate my Being,
May recognition come without dread or fear of being overwhelmed;

When the Divine Force of the celestial and fallen angels dawns upon
me,
May I receive help without fear, and recognize these visions as the
empty void.
When the Power of organic Karma evokes the dry metallic taste of
truth and illusion . . .
Dissipate the misery and suffering of heartburn,
When the Unveiled Kingdom reverberates like a thousand thunders,
Transmuted into the sounds of the six worlds of phenomena,
These six sounds close the door to rebirth in the Places of
Rebirth: 'OM' among the gods, 'MA' among the angels,
'ME' among the humans, 'TEG' among the sub-human heavy-jawed
brutes, 'MI' among the wandering insatiable spirits in the
ghost-world, and 'OM' among the dancing and joyfully
oblivious inhabitants of Hell.
Stripped of my mind and my Will-Power, and forced to follow the
reverberating momentum of organic karma,
I pray for the Compassionate angel of Grace to protect me,
When the Karmic habits and automatic mechanical activities of the
Organic World dawn upon me,
May the Five Elements, the Primary-Light-Formations of Earth, Air,
Fire, Water, and Ether, not rise up against me as my enemies
And may I not see them as enemies;
May I instead behold the Five Orders of french toast with maple syrup
at the home of The Never-Empty Coffee Cup.''

Offering this prayer in sincerity and humility, all fears and terrors disappear, and Liberation is attained. Believe it or not, the quality of sincerity, whether you mean it or not, is the most important factor at this moment.

the Vision of the Red Deer Goddess, driving a station wagon with a human tied across the fender

Undistracted by anything proceeding within you or around you, concentrate your effort and attention on this prayer and repeat it at least three times.

However weak your remaining organic Karma may be, Liberation can still be attained even though you have wandered very far down and are about to enter into the Third Level, where you might, against all odds, consciously pass the veil into the Unveiled Kingdom.

To those who have meditated often during their lifetime, the illusions at the moment of death are soon overcome and the Truth dawns on them at the moment of separation from the body.

The experience of the Clear Light while in the grip of organic illusion can't be stressed enough.

Those who have penetrated the visions of beingness, identity and nature are usually able to obtain great power during the Moments of Death, when the Clear Light dawns on them.

They welcome the Unveiled Kingdom as a friend with whom they are very familiar, and merge easily with it. This will be of great benefit while living in a material body.

Read these instructions regularly, allowing the meanings of the words to form in you the visions and then the penetration of the visions of phenomena, and remember that all visions are in reality the Transparent, Endless, Self-luminous Void of the Unveiled Kingdom.

The words and their hidden meanings will never be forgotten in the Place of Revealing, and seldom remembered in the Place of Hiding.

Even those who have committed the Five Unforgiveable Sins, the sins of Patricide, Matricide, setting two Elks' Lodges at war with one another, killing a Saint, and causing blood to flow from the body of the Man on the Cross, can be Liberated.

Get out there and form vast congregations. Heal the dead, raise the sick, cast out lepers!

There they are! Billions and billions of lost souls crawling around in the mud, just dying for your prayers and help! How can you just sit around here in the Unveiled Kingdom all day long, allowing them to remain immersed in the dark side of the veil? How can you let them suffer one moment longer?

$ $ $

No matter how disgusting,
grotesque,
foul,
filthy,
nauseating,
nasty,
gruesome,
putrid,
or revolting *these visions may be, they lose their
power over you the moment you send in that check
or money order for your mail-order course,*

**How I Raised Myself From the Dead
in 49 Days Or Less At Home in My
Spare Time And You Can, Too**

$ $ $

Preliminary Instructions

This is the Book of Rebirth, which contains specific instructions for choosing a suitable womb and closing a womb door should it prove unsuitable.

In choosing rebirth, a very high being who is about to be reborn will regard any passionate or aggressive parental sexual game as an indication of an unsuitable womb, but an interesting and instructive demonstration of unconscious but pleasant, satisfactions, generally completely recreational, genital sex.

A conscious rebirth is selected by calm and centered cooperative breathing as the couple seeks to immerse themselves in a single being formed in the Divine Embrace known as the Endless Knot.

This form of union is easily visible and discernible in the lucid knowingness during voluntary and intentional re-entry into the web of phenomenal visions.

The depth and elaboration of the vision of rebirth reverie should also be visible in your present state of clarity if you're paying more attention to the couple's state than to their activities.

The method of selecting rebirth is made easier by the clarified state which becomes obvious during the third stage in which visions of rebirth become dominant. Choosing one particular lifetime over another is made easy by the cheerful and cooperative angelic guide, who presents several options for spiritual evolution through visions similar to jukebox selections.

You might prefer to select a lifetime containing fewer painful experiences, but if you're smart, you'll select by evolutionary potential, not by avoidance of yucky experiences.

There they are! *Billions and billions of lost souls crawling around in the mud, just dying for your prayers and help!*

The real difficulty in the third stage of rebirth is to shut the door in wombs that you don't wish to enter, because the visions are confused and wombs seem to be ordinary inanimate objects, such as a cup, a fuzzy sweater, or even something completely subtle, like a gondola on the vaginal canal.

The principle instructions in the third stage are designed to help you to close the womb door to an unsuitable womb, and to discern the difference between an evolutionary womb and an involutionary womb, even though in this state they don't look like wombs. As a matter of fact, they could look like any ordinary object.

Choosing Rebirth
Guilding In:
The Selection of a Womb

Golly, it *has* been difficult for you, hasn't it? You've been asleep and fallen into the belief that it was all just a dream, haven't you? Well, then, listen carefully and try to understand what is happening to you even if it don't seem real ...

You have just had the Complete Guided Tour of Nothingness, during which your attention became fascinated by the visions of the primal elements of the Void, rooted to that endless primal slime we call "home" ... that eternal and infinite transparent jelly extending endlessly outward in a veritable crescendo of subtly shifting patterns of Bubbly Goo.

your recent passage through the phenomenal world.

When you suddenly found yourself free from the compelling power of the organic visions, you may have realized that you were able to function with supernormal powers and clarity, quickly discovering that you had a body similar to that of a living human being.

O, Adam, Son of Adam, you who will never taste the sweet pleasure of the forgetfulness of annihilation which is granted to all organic creatures, soon you may *wish* you could plunge yourself into the deep forgetfulness of organic death, madness, or eat a chocolate mousse.

With vision and sensation intact,
Wandering through endless
  endlessness,
You have the power to change the
  dream,
Being both the dream and the
  dreamer.

If you're smart, you'll select by evolutionary potential, not by the avoidance of yucky *experiences.*

It's hardly worth mentioning and probably an insult to your intelligence that the visions you've been experiencing were in fact the basic components of pure consciousness itself, automatically invoked by the reverberations of organic momentum which still clung to you after

Even though you can't die any more than you already have, it doesn't mean you can't feel sensations, just as the destructible and corruptible material body could.

As a matter of fact, since you no longer have a threshold for sensation governed by the organic body, even *more* sensation, perhaps more than you thought you could ever endure, will soon dawn upon you, if it hasn't already.

After a while you could get used to it, but unfortunately, that isn't too likely, as your consciousness is even now re-forming a new set of phenomenal visionsnionsness...

If your consciousness forms god visions, you'll be born in the world of gods. If it produces the visions of an angelic chamber, then you'll be born into the angelic world, and so on, depending on chance, some influence of the forces of habit, and the whims of the Olympian Gods. You'll be hearing several extremely suspicious sales pitches on the merits of various lifetimes, and you'll have to make a decision rather quickly, so be prepared to make a selection based on a fast-breaking series of visions of rebirth. Once the rebirth process begins, you won't have a chance to reconsider.

Depending on your inclinations, desires, beliefs and tendencies, you'll probably end up with some sort of compromise between horrible experiences in a highly evolutionary rebirth, and pleasant but recreational experiences in an evolutionarily useless rebirth.

Whatever you think you see, don't allow yourself to be drawn into a state of desire or resistance, or you'll be sucked down into rebirth in the pumpkin field of phenomenal visions before you have another chance to free yourself from its grip.

Death is just nature's way of telling you to slow down so you have a chance to penetrate all those visions you've been having.

Let the voidness of your consciousness fold and unfold once again. If you are able to relax and let yourself be the pure luminous, non-located unveiled vision of the endless Void in a state of non-action, without trying to reach for or withdraw from anything or hold on to anything you think you need in order to stabilize yourself, then you can still attain spontaneous liberation even at this stage of the game, and you won't have to be reborn as a toad.

If you're still having trouble realizing that all this is your own consciousness displayed for your enjoyment and indifferent amusement, then just try visualizing the angelic guide floating above you, and get into a state of non-attached devotion but watch out for falling angel-hair.

Don't just say, *I don't care —* *Anywhere but Here!*

It's very important that you make some effort to select an evolutionary rebirth at this stage, otherwise your resistance will be reproduced photographically, and you won't be able to stop rebirth. Don't allow yourself to wander, to fall into lethargy, apathy, euphoria or the Bijou Theater at this point, or you'll want to surrender, which may have been a terrific idea a few visions ago, but now it's not, so if possible, try to regain your sense of humor about your next organic you-know-what.

Congratulations. You can now take miraculous actions, assume various organic and nonorganic forms, and hallucinate in solid three-dimensional organic visions, complete with sensations and false memories, without limitations anywhere in the Six Phenomenal Worlds at no extra cost.

solidly engulfed within conditioned-organic visions.

Where do you want to go? What do you want to do? Don't just say, 'I don't care — Anywhere but Here!' Ask for spontaneous liberation in the pure realm of the Unveiled Vision...take a conscious rebirth, after which you will be able to work on your spiritual evolution, not as an Acid-Head in the Hashbury District of San Francisco.

Goolly, it hass been difficult for you, hasn't it?

Your activities are under the power of your habits, and so any habitual karma you have will spontaneously transport you to one or another bizarre space and time in Creation.

This can actually work wonders for you, evolutionarily speaking, because these instructions might by suggestion move you toward visions indicated as desirable, and away from those designated as undesirable.

You mustn't resist or become cynical about what I'm doing to help you. My voice can direct you just as a small child is able to attract a Great White Shark in the ocean, yet, if it were on land, he wouldn't be able to move it at all.

Here, in this state, your position is moveable and fluid, where in the phenomenal world you were unmoveable,

If you give in to your fears of humiliation or freak out at the strange sensations, or if your pride and vanity prevent you from abasing yourself and asking for help with humility and impersonal impartiality toward your identity, dignity, and the Santa Fe, then you'll get a random digital rebirth based on karmic accumulations, habits and rancid fats.

You ought to be able to endure this long enough to select a good rebirth. Even the sensations of The Two Headed Chamber can be endured for a *few* lousy moments. Concentrate on rebirth in the Realm of the Pure Clear Light, or if you're not ready for prime-time, then at least choose rebirth in The School so that you can learn and practice the teaching and donate heavily to our Self-Sufficient

Community Land Project. Then maybe this won't happen to you again so badly the next time.

Your present total freedom of movement through the Six Phenomenal Worlds is a sure sign that you are in the stage of rebirth, the re-formation of phenomenal consciousness.

This is a good time to remember what you learned from your modest jaunt through the Eternal World...

You now possess supernatural powers which can alter your subjective reality, but don't get hung up in these powers. They can alter specific visions within the dream in one way or another, but they don't change the situation.

In fact, they can make it worse by disguising reality as something more pleasant, but ultimately you will just trip down another primrose path to yet another dead end...so to speak.

previous lifetime as if you were there with them once again, but no matter what you do or say, they won't respond. Trying to get them to respond may get you into a worse condition than you are already. Any attempt to influence them or communicate with them could cause recurrence, trapping you once again as a ghost, haunting your former body.

You might be feeling regret at the loss of all that you had accumulated in that lifetime, but it's important to let go of whatever you once were, or believed yourself to be.

Your path is now strongly set for rebirth, and you'll feel driven by a powerful force within you, like an irresistible fart propelling you forward. That's the karmic wind of organic compulsions, cravings, and hungers, which are the underlying cause of all your subjective attractions and repulsions.

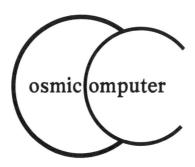

osmic omputer

You may begin to encounter those kindred spirits and partially developed souls who are going to be reborn with you in one or another of the lower worlds.

From here you should now be able to see your family, friends and home of your

There might be some confusion about what's happening to you because it will all seem so *ordinary* and yet, somehow strange.

You will imagine that you are being observed by inanimate objects. Don't be afraid; it's just your own paranoia that those against whom you committed what you consider to be negative acts will catch up with you while you're in this vulnerable condition, and of course, the feeling of being observed by inanimate objects, most of whom are at least ten times smarter than you've ever been.

You will feel as if a great disaster is about to happen...earthquakes, floods, fires, or the explosion of hydrogen bombs.

Nothing to worry about. These are only the results of tendencies of aggression, passion, and ignorance in your partially-reformed consciousness.

When all this starts happening, just try to penetrate these visions to the Clear Light, the Endless Creator, and pray in this way:

"*Please* don't let me forget what's
  really happening!
Don't allow me to fall into the pit of
  hell once again!
If you can't get me out of this, at least
  get me to a good rebirth
Where I can work on dumping these
  unconscious habits of organic life
  which seem to persist...
Oh, no...I just remembered...I *am*
  the pure luminous Void...
So to whom am I supposed to be
  praying, and to whom have I
  been praying all this time?"

If you have been practicing the teaching during your organic life and have accumulated habits of the Eternal World, you won't have a bad rebirth. Actually, you'll be feeling rather good

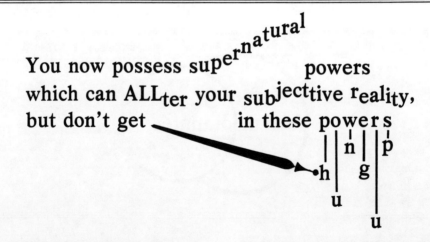

You now possess super natural powers which can ALLter your subjecttive reality, but don't get hung up in these powers

about your situation just about now. But if you have been indifferent toward the teaching during life, you will now see ugliness and ignorance all around you.

If you see objects of pleasure and desire, don't try to go after them, or attract them to you. You won't have to pay tax on these visions, because they aren't for resale.

Assume a state of indifference and pay attention to these instructions word-by-word.

you'll want to run or wander from chamber to chamber. You'll feel as if you're about to be captured. If you want to crawl into a safe space where you can be alone and get some rest, don't allow yourself to fall into this desperation to find a safe space. If you don't panic, you can avoid rebirth in a lower world.

None of the seemingly safe spaces

Here, in this state, your position is moveable and fluid, where in the phenomenal world you were unmoveable, $_e$S$_n$O$_g$L$_u$I$_l$D$_f$L$_e$Y$_d$ CON$_w$D$_i$I$_t$T$_h$I$_i$O$_n$NED- organic *VISIONS*

This is the Grand Tour of Safe Places, Solid Forms, and Shelters of Refuge. You'll see nice safe buildings, tunnels, caves, shrines, temples, monasteries, palaces, rocks, trees, boxes and warm clothing.

Anything solid and seemingly safe should be treated with suspicion. They're traps, forms which lead to automatic organic rebirth. You may feel the sudden impulse to become a statue or a rock. But don't give in to this kinky temptation.

You won't be able to grasp your fleeting attention as the passing thoughts flow faster and faster, and you'll no longer be able to see how they string together or what their sequence means. Everything will seem isolated, disconnected and out of context.

You'll be feeling hungry and tired and

you're seeing are actually as they appear to be. Look carefully at their color, and you'll be able to tell which world you're being attracted to.

At this point you might feel apprehension — perhaps that you're about to be the victim of some kind of attack — perhaps hunters, or a killer who's after you, always *has* been after you and has finally caught up with you, or a circle of evil witches trying to destroy you with spells, or federal agents closing in on you in low-flying helicopters at twelve-hundred dollars an hour in fuel bills, or the bogeyperson waiting to pounce on you and gobble you up.

But the fact is that it's your own show. No one is trying to do anything to you. You're the victim of a bad case of pantheism.

Just recall all the things that you consider good that you've ever done, and then all the things that you consider bad that you've ever done, and compare them, justifying all these actions which you're convinced you initiated.

thinking about all the things you've done, and you start evaluating them in values of right and wrong. All your worst fears seem to be coming true. Suddenly, you may think of me as the Lord of Death, the Monkey Man, the Gorilla your Dreams,

When there's no more struggle to

be have or *do*

you will find yourself awake.

Because you have forgotten the dream-machine nature of the world, you think that you're a specific identity with a will of your own. You've become hung up in the ability to alter action in the world, and the desire to think of something different to have happen other than what's happening. In the pureness of the Void, I told you what you could do . . . this is not all there is.

The fallen angel will now seem threatening to you. He'll gently inquire if anything's wrong, while you shake and shiver. You're sure he's *really* asking if you've *done* something wrong. If you can't tell him that you're afraid and that you don't know what's going on, you'll have to go through the next little drama. Because of pride, you get the booby-prize for your firm belief in the self.

You protest that you haven't done anything wrong. Suddenly you begin

the Crazy Clown. Look into the mirror; the Cosmic Computer.

At this point you're going to get *exactly* what you expected. This is just your expectation. Your karmic tendencies are bringing all this about. You could be spontaneously liberated right here and now, if you can see that you're the one who controls your own trip.

If, on the other hand, you're really heavily identified with this heavy drama, then the next step is inevitable. After all, why *shouldn't* you be the fall guy this time? Isn't that exactly what you've been doing to others?

What do you want me to do? Tie you up with a rope made of your own guts and drag you around? Suppose I cut your head off, tore out your heart, pulled out the remainder of your intestines, drank your blood, ate your brains, skinned you and ate the flesh, and then gnawed on the bones? If this isn't enough to remove your feelings of imaginary guilt, I could also plague you with bad puns while I'm doing it.

Uh, oh . . . It's happening again, and after I told you to be careful. Well, that'll teach you to stay awake. Sure is an *accommodating* universe, isn't it? No matter how many times this happens, you manage to recover, being unborn and all, but even though you can't die, you can feel pain.

If you could only realize that you are the shining and luminous Void, none of this would have to happen. I hate to say 'I told you so' but I told you so.

After you get the punishment you think you deserve for being such a rotten kid, a great emptiness — as if a huge weight had been lifted from you — will come over you . . . not the absence of somethingness, but the awe-inspiring endless emptiness of the Void, than which there has never been anything but.

Even this voice is the Void. Always has been.

See this emptiness as your own endless nature, defining the point of no return on sale items or damaged goods, where the sentient beings who are liberated and those who plunge headfirst into rebirth are separated.

Don't allow yourself to become confused by the pandemonium shadow-show going on around you. If you give up now and fall asleep, you'll be carried down, down, down . . . into the wheel of karma, beyond any chance of instant liberation.

If you fall into euphoria, you won't be able to attain spontaneous liberation just by hearing and recognizing the visions as imaginary forms of the Unveiled Vision.

If you can't handle it here, just see my form as a pleasant and safe being who wants to help you get free of this endless round of death and rebirth for a modest fee. You are going to be tossed around between states of joy and sadness alternating in each moment. Don't try to resist or give in to blissful sleep or dull, grinding passion.

If you decide to take rebirth in one of the higher realms and your previous relatives or friends want you to go to the Protestant Heaven instead, don't express anger or resentment toward them or try to get them to stop using chemical mouthwash and deodorant soap. Just let them do what they're doing, and be here.

Now we'll see just how impartial to

At this point you're going to get *exactly* what you expected. This is just your expectation. Your karmic tendencies are bringing all this about. You could be spontaneously liberated right here and now, if you see that you're the one who controls your own trip.

your previous life you really are. If you feel any anger or resentment toward their displeasing manifestations, you'll be drawn back into the old life, or reborn as a transvestite den-mother in Albuquerque, New Mexico.

If you're still attached to any of the people or possessions you left behind in the life you were just doing, or if you feel attached to what you accumulated and you get angry or upset about losing it, even momentarily, it could draw you down into the world of insatiable spirits or the hell world, even if you were just about to be reborn in a higher state like Maine or New Hampshire.

It can cost you very dearly to be

unless you take rebirth as what you were before. That old black magic is behind you now. You don't want to return to it again, do you?

While I'm delivering these instructions for you to use in self-guidance toward an evolutionary rebirth, as you listen through the ethers, as a result of impure thoughts and perceptions arising from your karmic tendencies, you may feel that I'm reading carelessly, stupidly, sleepily, inattentively, without any real intention or interest in your condition, and you may feel betrayed or upset, and become upset or angry at me for not performing these actions correctly or exactly.

Sure is an
acc
acco
accomm
accommo

DATING UNIVERSE,

Isn' *TiT?*

attached to anything you left behind, or to resist anything that's coming, so be careful to untie the rope before you leave the dock, or you'll end up as just another face on the cutting room floor.

Even if you hated to leave your buddies behind, you can't have them back from the front. You can't get to them

If you become upset with me for not performing these functions properly, you have forgotten that this is your trip and that I'm simply acting out my part in your drama! If you think you can do any better, buy your own copy of *The Lazy Man's Guide To Death and Dying*, and read it yourself!

Observing the community of human beings, don't think that they are your personal friends. You've been living among the pure shining luminous Void, and if anyone is doing anything right or wrong, it's *your own* idea of right and wrong, left and right, up and down, in and out, Past and Future, Gallagher and Sheen, Scratch n' Sniff, Punch and Judy, Happy and Sad, Sea and Ski...

No matter how you're seeing it, everyone is acting and performing exactly according to law, no matter how it seems to you.

All of us practitioners do our job with pure devotion and actions, because everyone here is part of the Unveiled Vision, and we work for minimum wage.

There's no one here but us dimensional, tactile hallucinations. I mean, you stare at *anything* long enough, and it'll start moving.

Spots on the *wall* will talk to you after a while! It's when they begin to make *sense* that you should worry. And when you start talking back to them, trying to reason with a speck of fly doo-doo, then you know you've gone off the deep end...

Speaking of fly doo-doo, it may have become apparent to you by now that there are three different types of perception or awareness as you pass through the Unveiled Vision of the Nonphenomenal World...

In the first stage, as you try to create the Creation, you can safely respond to the visions exactly as they appear to you.

In the second stage, trying to destroy the Creation, you can trust the visions to behave as if true...

But in this third stage, creating the imaginary *absence* of the eternal Creation, you can't trust the visions to be as they appear, because they have been created to hide the Creation *as if it didn't exist.*

In order to avoid a Lesser Arcana rebirth, you will have to either recognize that anything you see is in fact the Unveiled Kingdom, or else you'll have to decode the real meaning behind each of the visions you see before you as they dawn upon you and not a moment later.

You've probably noticed by now that you're being pushed from behind into a restless wandering by a steady and compelling force.

You may feel as if you are being hunted by something horrible, like a gorilla, or a fierce animal, or a pack of hunters, or perhaps an insane blond-eyed, blue-haired clown. You may feel the urge to push, but don't.

Transform these feelings and sensations into beneficent friendly apparitions devoid of realness other than the form and force you provide them with by your reactions, if you'll pardon my dangling participle.

Then let the sinking sensations of ironic laughter dissolve slowly from the edges inward, and place your attention firmly on what is left after it has vanished.

Take a deep cleansing breath and begin with me the emergency prayer for closing the womb door:

"Now that the rebirth of my phenomenal
consciousness is happening to me,
I concentrate without distraction and,
striving to maintain good karma,
I close the door of the private womb
without resistance, and do not enter.
Now is the time for pure thought and
impartial emotion!
I abandon desire and jealousy and
meditate on a ham sandwich and a
cool can of beer.
This is what you call a prayer for closing
the womb door?"

That was a very good prayer. You
should have closed just about every
womb door in sight with that little
blockbuster.

Now you are at the threshhold
between involution and evolution, between the high and the low. If you fall
asleep here even for a single moment you
will be reborn without choice of race,
breed, color, sex or tax-bracket.

If on the sound of my voice giving
these instructions, your consciousness is
concentrated, the time has come to learn
the Five Foolproof Methods for closing
the womb door. Hey! This could easily be
your last chance to gas up before crossing
the great empty desert of rebirth.

If you see couples making love, don't
try to pry them apart with a silver-
handled walking-stick!

Mentally prostate your glands before
these angelic guides with deep diversion
and serious reservations.

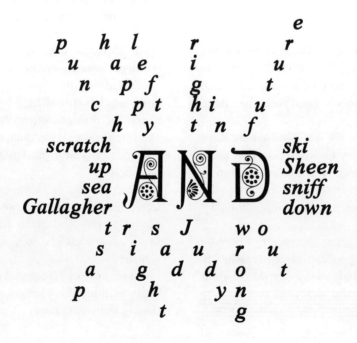

Ask them for the method of obtaining the teachings of self-evolution!

Then ask them for help in obtaining a good rebirth in a school where you can practice the teachings and at the same time get a terrific tan!

Now ask them for a pencil and paper so you can take notes on their lovemaking technique!

Suddenly the door to rebirth will close, because they will ask you to kindly leave the womb!

What a great method of closing the womb!

But if that doesn't work, then you'll continue your plunge into rebirth. Now listen carefully. Here's the second method of closing the womb door...

If you are about to be born as a male, you'll feel jealousy toward the Father and desire for the Mother.

If, on the other hand, you are about to be born as a female, you'll feel envy and jealousy toward the Mother and passion and desire toward the Father, unless you're about to be reborn into a gay family in or near San Francisco, in which case you'll feel envy and jealousy toward both the father and the mother, and passion and desire toward yourself.

These Passions will cause you to be reborn by drawing you through the womb door, and you will experience the bliss of relief from the fears and terrors of the sensations and force which drove you toward rebirth.

You might try to hide between the sperm and the ovum, but once again, your perceptions can't be trusted, so you'll probably think you're hiding between two trees, inside a cave, lying down on or in a bed, or having sex with a member of your own or an unrelated species.

---

invocational prayer,

Get me out of this any way you can!

After the fusion of the sperm and ovum, you may lose consciousness until the beginning of the process of rebirth...unless you can, through special tactile hallucination penetration techniques acquired at special weekend workshops, remain fully conscious while in the womb.

If you haven't had our special tactile hallucination workshops, you'll probably sleep deeply until the head is engaged or even when it's just going steady in the birth-canal and then, as you enter the new life, you will be lost on the wheel of phenomenal activities and organic habits once again, tormented by needless suffering, constantly dramatizing the events and visions which caused fear, and by the singing of the boatmen in the birth-canal.

You'll see visions of invaders from outer space, extra-sensory perception, supernatural phenomena and you'll receive psycho-somatic implants to become a post-natal vegetarian.

When your passions and aggressions conspire together to influence you toward vegetarianism, just pray sincerely in this way:

"Alas and alack! I have such powerful organic karma that
   I've wandered all the way down until here I am,
   wondering whether or not to become a vegetarian!
It's obvious to me now that I'm in this situation because
   I've been clinging to passion, aggression and
   personalized stationery.
Wandering endlessly in the Six Worlds of phenomenal
   visions,
Sinking beneath the sea of misery for a long long time,
I resolve to do something or other . . . to . . . to . . .
I forget just what, but I definitely resolve to do
   something, whatever it was . . .
Trying to always have it my way has only brought me
   torment, pain, and fast-food-dyspepsia.
Therefore I will never again allow myself to . . .
I still can't remember what . . . but whatever it was, I
   resolve never again to do it!"

If you have concentrated your full attention and
sincerity on this prayer, you have just moments left in
which to change your mind . . .

If the womb remains open, and you are about to enter,
then it can still be closed by the next instruction on the
illusory nature of all experience. Form your considera-
tions in this way:

"No matter what I think is happening or what I think I
   see, I am the Unveiled Kingdom.
The visions of the womb, the storms, the rolling
   thunder, the whirlwind, the terrifying apparitions of
   angels and demons, and my sensations of fear are just
   subjective forms of my own consciousness, folding and
   unfolding.

The only genuine experience I have ever had is that of
the Unveiled Kingdom, before all the visions began.

No matter how it seems, the unveiled vision is the only
reality. Only the unveiled vision am real.

What good am it to desire an empty and unreal illusion?

What good do it do me to cling to an apparition as if it
were solid? What am I skeered of? There is naught but
the Clear Shining Light, and so nothing can harm me,
with Daddy and Mammy standing by . . .

Can it be that I need to exist so desperately that I am
willing to do all this to myself?

Can it be that every vision I see am simply the Void?
Then there ain't no sense clinging to them. Even the
voidness of the Void is nonexistent in reality, and has
been nonexistent from the very beginning.

Even this here voice, this teaching and the necessity for
instructions on penetrating the visions and sensations
am non-existent, although the book are objectively
real and worth ten times the cover price.

There never were, nor will there was, a ''world of
phenomena'', nor was there ever been or will there is
''Six Worlds'' in which to take rebirth.

I have been walking in a dream, struggling as if there
were something to resist, but I've just drawn the net
more tightly around myself like as if I was struggling
against a Chinese finger-puzzle.

I resist no longer. No self, no void, no wombs, no male,
no female, no death, no rebirth, no reality, no
unreality . . .

Only my own endless endlessness with no beginning
and no end.

Now I am finished with desire, aggression, resistance,
attractions, thoughts, experience.

I yam what I yam. No other, there ain't.''

By concentrating the full force of one's attention on this prayer and disallowing the consciousness to form itself into a specific identity, the reality of the womb and the struggle to resist rebirth vanish in a puff of smoke.

When all belief in the phenomenal self is destroyed, there *is* nothing to be reborn. If you can bring yourself to renounce *all* experience, not only thoughts, feelings, sensations and activities, but even pure beingness without form and substance, then all womb doors will certainly be closed and there will be no rebirth.

But if, after all this, the womb entrance still isn't closed and the belief in experience and existence can't be dissolved...if you still insist on being someone or something in particular, then have I got another instruction for you!

All substances, visions, sensations and experiences are your own projected forms of consciousness. This consciousness is the uncreated unborn emptiness of the endless Luminous Crystal Light of the Void in infinite extension, without center, without circumference; without beginning, without end, and without middle.

As you concentrate on this idea, allow your thoughts to flow naturally, as industrial sewage flows into the pure water of the river. By allowing yourself to rest naturally in a silent meditation on industrial pollution, you can be sure that the revolving door to rebirth in the atmosphere of sodium glare will be closed.

Spots on the *wall* will talk to you after a while! It's when they begin to make

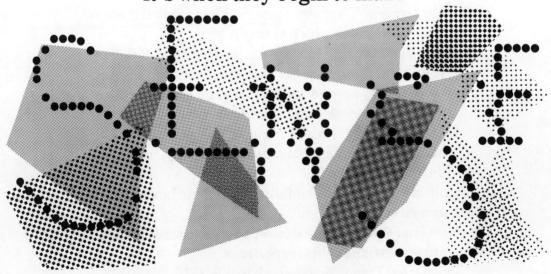

that you should worry

Now I've given you all five methods for closing the womb door, and it's rare that an individual doesn't attain spontaneous liberation through one or another of these methods.

Your present consciousness has the ability to hear and understand this teaching, even if, when under the influence of organic phenomena, all this stuff sounds like so much meaningless gobbledegook.

All your perceptions and sensations are now intact as if they were never impaired during your previous lifetime.

If you were overcome by fear, maybe now you'll be willing to listen to a few suggestions.

You ought to be able to hear, understand and follow the instructions I give you, however, because as the free consciousness has no roots or anchor points it will be naturally attracted to any area of attention to which it is directed by these instructions, and repelled just as easily from anything which it's directed to resist.

Just as a boulder which was impossible to move on land even with a boulder sling can be moved when it's in the water with one finger if the finger is sufficiently large, so are you able to be moved in the water of the endless Void, and therefore your presence is fluid and extremely easy to guide by voice, even easier than a boulder is guided when a ninety-eight pound wench moves a lumberjack.

Therefore, it's important to direct the attention at every stage, not just one or two, in order to indicate the places and methods of liberation, if not at one stage, then at another, and if not at that stage,

then at another; and if not at that stage, then another. That's one reason why so many confrontations with the unveiled vision are given so many times in so many forms and variations, however repetitively redundant it may be. And if not repetitively redundant, then unnecessarily restated . . . another reason for this is that I get paid by the word.

Many voyagers come this way who aren't interested in liberation and meet this teaching with disinterest. They think this stuff is boring. If you asked them to describe this teaching in one word, "boring" would spring to their lips. They go on and on about how boring this teaching is . . .

I don't think it's boring. I don't think this teaching is boring at all. As far as I'm concerned, it's really quite exciting. You will often hear voyagers remarking on how exciting it is. *They* don't think it's boring. The only ones who think it's boring are those who only know how to produce suffering in and around themselves because they feel suffering and don't know how to make the efforts necessary to liberate themselves from suffering.

They prefer to wander in the Six Worlds rather than face the terrifying simplicity of the unveiled vision, and so they produce the elaborate intricacies which cause mental phenomena just so they can maintain the confusions, distractions, drives, urges, cravings, aberrations, necessities, significances, purposes, goals, aims, needs, problems, and continuous occupation with the boring business of organic survival.

On the other hand, the effort to

awaken is just another game designed to maintain sleep. There isn't any specific effort that must be made in order to awaken. In fact, it's just the opposite.

I suggest you stop making efforts to remain asleep and simply cease to have anything to do with action and reaction. Don't try to make anything happen or not happen.

Let go of your efforts to maintain consciousness and reality. Automatically as those drop away you will be the only

Don't allow yourself to drift off or to fall asleep. Repeat this instruction with me and guide your thoughts along this path:

**"I take refuge in the Clear Light.
I take refuge in the angel of mercy and compassion.
I take refuge in the Way of the Teaching.
I take refuge in the company of evolved Spiritual Souls."**

I **YAM** WHAT I **YAM**.

reality remaining. When there's no more struggle to *be* something, *have* something, or *do* something, you will find yourself awake.

Even those who are grimly playing the deadly serious game of organic existence can still be liberated — even here — if they will only listen to this emergency instruction, so pay close attention and try to follow it exactly.

If you can ask for help sincerely without a sigh of infinite boredom, a whimper of lingering fear, or a flinch of personal humiliation, you can attain liberation by taking refuge in the One who am the source of this here Great Liberating Teaching, who receives no royalties on the sale of this book, who gets no credit for being the real author . . . but who's complaining?

the present **IS** the destination

How to Choose Rebirth Without Really Trying

Even though you've been given many wonderful instructions on how to spontaneously liberate yourself, you haven't yet crossed over the line, and so the womb door hasn't closed and you are definitely about to take rebirth.

As long as it's inevitable anyway, I don't feel that there's anything to lose by providing you with several instructions on how to choose a specific rebirth by womb selection, so listen carefully, and don't allow your fantasy-prone attention to wander any further down the line than it already has.

The signs of birth are about to appear. Remember, the worlds are color-coded for easy reference and identification, so you should be aware of the color as well as the form.

Pay attention to details, and you'll be able to gather all the information you need in order to choose well. Details are more important than gross forms.

If you see a lake with white water-cranes on it, don't go there. It's strictly for the birds, so you should avoid it.

If you see a huge mansion of very high aesthetic design, enter there, if you happen to have the price of admission burning a hole in your nonphenomenal pockets. When you've got it, flaunt it.

If you see a huge pile of horse manure, even though you could fulfill your cravings for pleasure there, it's a non-evolutionary place of rebirth, and

there's no guarantee that there's a pony somewhere around, just because there's a mound of horseshit.

If you see a lake with cattle, even though you could have a long and peaceful life there, spiritual evolution is not available in a dairy barn, although it might be available on the haystack in back of the barn.

If you see soft white temples and highly simplified, well-designed buildings on hilltops, or a miserable urban apartment in which fifty to a hundred people are crammed sitting in various uncomfortable postures and balancing paper plates with Western Asiatic foods on their laps, then you're going to be born into The Work. Enter there if you can find a place to sit. That's our school!

If you see glades with large ferns, or beautiful groves of small leafed trees and winding streams or tight small wheels of fire looking like slowly revolving pinwheels don't get attracted to it. Feel revulsion and disgust toward it. That's *their* school.

If you see caves and holes in the ground or under hills as if through a foggy mist, don't enter there. You may also see straw huts, wooden shacks, or abandoned railroad cars and engine barns, or dark hallways and dead-end chambers. Don't dodge in there, no matter *what* seems to be chasing you, unless it's something scary...

If you see treestumps, charred black shapes sticking up from the ground, shallow caves and patches of burnt ground, then get the sensations of unbearable hunger and thirst, and you'll be able to resist it. Feel intense disgust toward that landscape. Don't, under any circumstances, think of it as a place in which to hide. And don't run into any large black monoliths. If you fall asleep now, for you, the war is over.

If you hear or see military troops singing battle-songs such as "Heighdy, Heighdy, Heighdy Ho, I Got a Girl in Mexico..." as they march menacingly across a desolate and dark twisted country with houses of red and black, and there are black pits alongside the black road, rocky crags and slag heaps everywhere, and a black smoky cloud over everything, you're about to be born as an inhabitant of the hell world.

If you end up there you will be enslaved and made to attend stock-car races and labor grimly at the destruction of the land and subjugation of the other inhabitants.

There are tortures and inquisition, war and continual political and economic treachery. Machinery and engines producing foul gases are everywhere, and even if you try to die there, they have life-support devices to force you to survive even if you don't want to.

The hell world is so full of pain and horror that you might never regain your stability and equilibrium long enough to get out of it, so don't go near it at all, even in fascination that such a thing could exist.

Be careful. It's better to go anywhere rather than into the hell-world, unless you're an awakened being, in which case it doesn't matter where you are because no one vision is any more significant than any other.

But if you're not an awakened being, then you should arouse in yourself the

On the other hand, the effort to awaken is just another game designed to maintain sleep. There isn't any specific effort that must be made in order to awaken. In fact, it's just the opposite.

I suggest you stop making efforts to remain asleep and simply cease to have anything to do with action and reaction. Don't try to make anything happen or not happen.

Let go of your efforts to maintain consciousness and reality. Automatically as those drop away you will be the only reality remaining.

sensation of revulsion to its seductive magnetic force, at the same time maintaining your full attention, diffusing your vision to expand outward into the peripheral corners of the eyes.

Your fervent and powerful intention to stay away from the hell world is needed now. Don't fall asleep. Keep awake and resist with all your effort until the womb door to hell is closed.

Unfortunately your power to remain free of rebirth is now gone, so even if you don't wish rebirth you have no choice but to take rebirth somewhere or other... but it doesn't have to be in the hell world.

You will undoubtedly notice a peculiar force like a strong wind pushing you from behind.

This is the karmic wind, the force of organic habits which have continued by automatic momentum, forcing you to wander into rebirth of one kind or another.

Behind you are the visions and sensations that caused you to feel fear, and before you vast hordes of sadistic and degraded beings in hospital greens are eagerly awaiting your next rebirth.

I know it's hard to decide what's best. Confusion swirls all around you; everyone is shouting directions at you, telling you

you have to ask **directly** and **specifically** for help.

what to do, which rebirth to take, what's best for you, and making it impossible for you to orient yourself in order to choose wisely and carefully.

As you search frantically for some sort of refuge from all this confusion, perhaps you see some buildings or rocks, a cave, or a nice inviting bed, perhaps already inhabited by an even more inviting sexual partner...

Eventually you'll realize that you have wandered into a womb which you no doubt thought was something else entirely...

Your perceptions deceived you, but now you are afraid to come out, even though you still have a chance to escape because you're afraid that if you leave your safe space you'll be tortured and ripped apart by those sadistic and degraded beings, or that the great pumpkin will get you, so, however bad it may seem to take rebirth, you'll do it rather than face those hordes of demons, those hounds of hell, once again. Is that what you call a sense of humor?

If you want to destroy your tormentors, it's up to you.

Since they're your own subjective visions anyway, nothing could be easier. Simply visualize the angel of mercy as a huge and terrible chicken with four legs and a mouthful of teeth, towering over them in an attitude of wrath and anger.

The Chicken of Mercy will, by your command, proceed to crush all those evil forces into the ground, and then, while you're momentarily protected from these hordes of evil creatures, you should be able to take this opportunity to shop intelligently for a womb more or less at your leisure, and you'll have the time to make the proper choice according to your consumer needs.

All these sensations of fear have taken root through the power of your own beliefs and expectations. At this point probably the best thing you can do is to meditate on the Great Emptiness of the Unveiled Vision of the Kingdom of the Void of The Endless Non-Dimensional Self-Luminous Nonphenomenal Shining Clear Light, but if you can't seem to force yourself to make this comparatively

rampant alienation they haven't taken you away to the Home for the Mildly Irrational, and you still feel compelled by the karmic wind to wander into a womb, you might as well make the best of it, and here's how:

Okay...Because you've descended into the Third Stage, near the places of rebirth, but still far enough above them to exert some influence on the causal world, you now possess the supernatural power to know all the particulars of any single incarnation or lifetime.

The Chicken of Mercy will, by your command, proceed to **CRUSH** **evil** all those **GROUND** forces into the

minor effort, then at least take a rebirth in which you're forced to take a more challenging part in the organic drama that can produce the automatic necessity for transformation so that you can someday take your place in that great minority of turtles who work to support the Throne of Our Endless Creator.

If you can't work as a turtle, then just withdraw from the whole drama and say to yourself: This isn't happening. This has nothing to do with me. I quit from the whole thing. You guys carry on, but count me *out*.

If, after this momentary lapse into

You can use this opportunity to obtain a definite picture of the options and choices available to you. You should choose a lifetime for your next rebirth as if you were buying a house on a veteran's pension plan, or a used car from a dealer who does video advertising.

There are three upper births in the higher realms, and six lower births in the organic-phenomenal worlds. You might even be able to obtain a birth in the Clear Light. Let's see if it's possible...Try it with me. To obtain a free transfer to the Pure Realm of the Clear Shining Light, form your thoughts in this way:

"Alas, what a bummer. After all this time, floundering around in the stinking swamp of organic phenomena, after countless ages in the Eternal Creation, without beginning and without end, while so many others were able to liberate themselves, I haven't been able to even ask for help.

"Now I'm going to ask for help, even here in the place of rebirth. It's not too late even now. From this moment on, I feel sickened by the world of organic phenomena. There's nothing there for me. I don't want any part of it. There's nothing to learn there, nowhere to hide. I'm tired of cringing in the darkness and clinging to the endless parade of organic visions, fascinations and distractions.

"Now it's time for me to give up living in the Six Worlds, so I'm going to take spontaneous rebirth in the endlessly folding and unfolding Lotus Flower in the Pure, Endless Realm of The Clear Shining Light. I'm going to bathe in the Pure Light and allow it to wash away all this phenomenal filth that's been accumulating on me. I feel cleansed, now. I'm going...I'm going...I'm being reborn in the Realm of Luminous Clear Light. I can feel the purity. I can feel it. I can feel it. I'm going now."

If you're still hearing my voice, then that didn't work either. Damn. Now you'll have to follow the instruction for choosing an impure birth in one of the Six Lower Worlds. This isn't working out very well for you, is it? Well, hang on, third time's the charm.

If you start smelling something sickeningly sweet, then you're about to be born as a horsefly in a pile of dung. Whatever it looks like, if it smells sweet or looks foggy or cloudy, don't get near it. Back off, using the power of revulsion and disgust, and choose another womb entrance instead, unless spending a Saturday night as a horsefly in a pile of dung is your idea of a good time.

Repeat the following prayer along with me, to guide your thoughts:

"I will be reborn in the Work and for the Work of spiritual evolution, for the benefit of all beings everywhere.

"I take rebirth within the realm of the practice of the Teaching. I will take a body with merits and Grace which can be used for the benefit of all beings everywhere and for the Absolute, our Endless Creator.

"I will practice the teaching in my new life and during that lifetime I will perfect myself toward liberation so that all beings everywhere might benefit from my liberation in my next passage.

"Next time, I resolve not to die as unprepared as I was this time for liberation and awakening."

Concentrating fully on this intention will open a suitable womb. Immediately upon entering such a special womb, you should sanctify it and treat it as a temple dedicated to the self-luminous vision of the unveiled kingdom.

Ask for the teaching during that lifetime. It's within your power to direct the actions of the liberating angels to guide you toward spontaneous liberation, but you have to ask *directly* and *specifically* for help. If you can't ask for help, then you'll just have to suffer a few more turns through the meatgrinder until your vanity allows you to beg for mercy.

When you ask for help in pulling all your karma past, present and future into the present so it can all be handled in one single lifetime, allowing you to take your rightful place in the Work in which you participate as a functioning part of a circle of invocation which causes evolution automatically by radiation produced during periods of intentional labors of individuals working as a connected group resembling a whole functioning fallen

But to activate this process, you must *consciously* and *deliberately* ask for the process of dissolving the phenomenal veil. That's all there is to it . . .

If you can just allow the nonphenomenal presences of the periodic table of angels to dissolve by their very presence your mental distrust, organic sleep, unconscious actions, ego struggles, desires, attachments, passions, aggressions, pride, arrogance, cravings and organic habits and hungers, you're ready to begin to prepare for work in the Eternal World!

But if you're not an awakened being, then you should arouse in yourself the sensation of revulsion to its seductive magnetic force, at the same time maintaining your full attention, diffusing your vision to expand outward into the peripheral corners of the eyes.

---

angel, taking its place in the angelic chamber to which it was originally assigned, with the invocational prayer, **Get me out of this any way you can!**, the nonphenomenal guide is activated, which is to say, the exact component of your deepest consciousness which has the unique function of opening your eyes by dissolving the phenomenal veils — the safety factor that insures that you won't be liberated until you're ready for it — will begin to actively operate.

It's possible that a womb might seem good or bad, or you might have feelings of like or dislike about one womb or another.

Again, you can't trust your impressions in this stage and the great secret here is to remain perfectly impartial, in a state of high indifference. In this state of high indifference there is no good, no bad, no desire, no resistance, no approval, no disapproval, no passion, no disgust, no apathy, no aggression, no parking, no shirt, no service, no tickee, no washee.

If you can't let go, and you're still having trouble selecting a lifetime in the old jukebox of organic life, decide that, no matter what happens from now on, you'll concentrate your full attention on the Naked King, and hold the idea that all phenomenal visions are hallucinations, veils, illusions, which blanket the endless vision of the Naked King.

Give up your friends, your relations, your knowledge, your understanding of how it used to be, your influence, and your power.

Let go of all your material accumulations; you will get exactly what you need in this next lifetime, just as every chamber you passed through in the angelic world contained everything necessary for work within it.

I know it's going to be tough to break in a new organic body to your old karmic habits, but you're going to have to try to let go of your desire to get back your former body, because if you don't, you'll circle back around to the front door of that old mansion you just left, and go through it again.

You might feel tempted to recycle yourself back through the former life, but it's an obstruction on your path to liberation and awakening, and besides, we've already got it rented out on a seventy-six year lease.

Enter now into the blue light of the human world or the soft white light, leading to the jewelled temples and gardens of delight in the world of the gods.

The Confrontations while Experiencing Reality called the Teaching Which Liberates Just By Hearing and Which Liberates By Penetration Through Visions Until The Unveiled Kingdom Is Revealed By Sheer Grit and Stubborn Determination, completely disregarding all odds, is now completed.

T
h
i
There is no other teaching.
s
i
t
.

goodnight, Gracie

Afterword

Properly licensed ministers of this teaching who have kept their ordination certificates up to date automatically have the power to produce a permanent, instantaneous and spontaneous liberation before and during passage, during the visions, and in the state of rebirth.

Even the most miserable and conventional working stiff on the day-job market, and the most neurotic, pill-head-alcoholic-suburban-suddenly-single parent can attain spontaneous liberation—or a reasonable facsimile thereof—simply by mindlessly following these instructions and asking, without fear of personal humiliation, for help and guidance toward liberation in this lifetime. Not to worry, no salesperson will call.

So we see that it's possible for even the most vicious, violent, unconscious creature...even someone who sits on public toilet seats and screws everyone in sight, to be crammed with a shoehorn into a lifetime which provides the opportunity to receive the teaching even if they've done nothing to actually deserve it, but that this method is not effective until just before the entrance into a womb prior to rebirth.

This teaching is so profound that it can lead even the most evil and degraded being onto the secret path, but it can't make him drink.

During the next lifetime you should resolve to practice releasing your attachments, passions, aggressions and hungers for organic life and the pursuit of pleasure-sensations while you're still under the influence of organic sensations.

This is far better than seated meditations in a serene exterior-world environment.

If you can train yourself to remain inwardly serene while your organic machine is being mercilessly lashed with velvet whips and your headbrain is being devoured by hard-rock music at three thousand decibels, this instruction will certainly cause the veil to lift permanently at the moment before death, but of course, under those conditions, *anything* would!

There is no other teaching. This is it.

Don't forget that liberation is not necessarily awakening. It feels better, and enhances awakening, but after awakening you won't mind being where you are. To someone who is awake, the present *is* the destination, not some future event, real or imaginary.

Liberation makes the dream a whole lot better, and gives fast, fast relief from suffering. But real awakening is simply waking up and allowing the dream to go on, with you or without you. When you no longer feel the urge to manipulate the dream and make it better, you'll wake up. And when you wake up, you wake up.

This book should be proclaimed in the ears of all living persons everywhere; it should be read over the pillows of all persons who are ill, troubled, anxious, weird, freaky, or wishing instruction in the Art of Death and Dying; it should be read at the site of all corpses; it should be broadcast over the media of all nations. But most of all, it should be marketed at

When
you no
longer feel
the urge to
manipulate the
dream and make it
better,

you'll **Wake Up.**
And when

you **Wake Up,**

you **Wake Up.**

full retail, never remaindered or returned for credit.

This book is the description of the method of expanding consciousness to reach out over many bodies, times, conditions, deaths, and worlds. It is the method of Saint Buddha and his Bodhisattvas.

Liberation will be won simply by not disbelieving it when hearing it; giving it the benefit of the doubt is enough to be able to begin to hear and use this doctrine to attain spontaneous Liberation.

Disseminate this book. Sell it to a friend. Hearing it only once, even though one has no comprehension of the subject matter, or the meaning, it may be remembered by the being when it passes from this world.

May this book be of real benefit to all beings everywhere, and help to bring about the spontaneous liberation and real awakening of all. Good luck, and be sure to write if you get work.

The Author

Dear Reader of the *Lazy Man's Guide to Death & Dying:*

On the outside chance, a long shot I admit, that the reading of this book failed to produce the expected spontaneous liberation and reasonably perfect enlightenment, then perhaps you're ready for the 'not so lazy' man's intentional preparation for death and dying.
If so, write to:

I.D.H.H.B., Inc.
P.O. Box 370, Department L
Nevada City, CA 95959

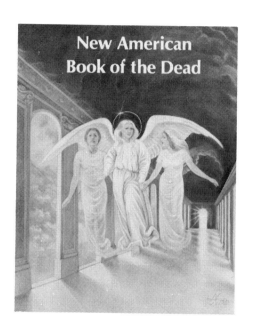

New American Book of the Dead

Available now in its 6th edition! Internationally recognized, the *New American Book of the Dead* is *the* text on reincarnation and the between-lives state. Now in a completely revised sixth edition, this version is the first *truly American* Book of the Dead, adapted to the Western Civilization. This edition includes information on how to use the book, interviews, and new Readings with Angelic Guides.

Read this book from cover to cover. I highly recommend it! — from the introduction by John C. Lilly, M.D., author of *Center of the Cyclone*.

Paperback, **$7.95**

How I Raised Myself From the Dead
[in 49 days or less]

Then I knew with a cold wave of certainty that I was going to have to leave everything behind me . . . my friends, my family, my home, my business, but most of all, my body which, in spite of everything, was home to me. I knew I couldn't take them with me where I was going, but somehow it didn't seem to really matter if any of it survived. From where I was at the time everything I had accumulated or accomplished in life was no more useful or important to me than something I had accomplished in a dream.

This authentic presentation of one individual's journey through the Transit experience is available once again on cassette tape! While listening to this tape try lying with eyes closed in a quiet space lit by candlelight.

Cassette Tape, **$9.95**